彩圖
聖經故事

My
Bible
Friends

CONTENT
目錄

小小嬰孩摩西
Baby Moses

小摩西一出生，就要被丟到河裏了。
因為邪惡的國王說，所有的男嬰統統都要丟到河裏！
可憐的小摩西該怎麼辦呢？

2

Moses was a wee baby boy.
His Mother loved him and held him close.
His Father loved him and patted his fat cheeks.
Sister Miriam loved him and sang him happy songs.
Little Brother loved him and tickled his tiny toes.
Never was a baby more loved than Baby Moses.

摩西是個剛出生的小男嬰。
媽媽疼他，把他緊緊摟在懷裏。
爸爸疼他，輕輕拍他圓嘟嘟的小臉蛋。
姐姐米利暗疼他，唱快樂的歌給他聽。
小哥哥也愛他，喜歡搔癢他的小腳趾。
從來沒有別的寶寶像小摩西一樣，受到這麼多的疼愛。

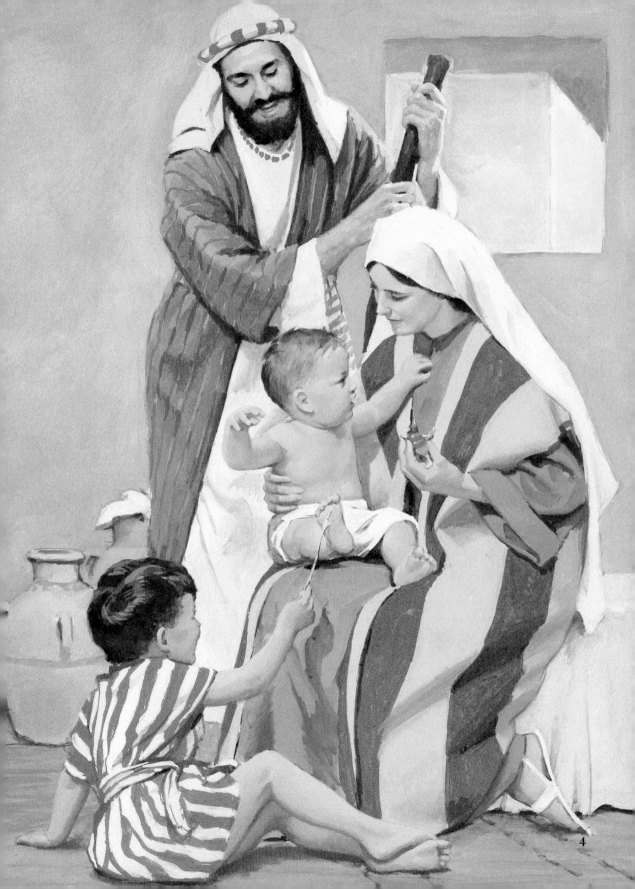

4

5

But the king where Moses lived was a wicked man.
He said to his helpers,
    "Throw all the baby boys into the river."
"Oh, no, no!" said Mother, and held Baby Moses closer.
"We'll never let anyone throw our baby into the river," said Father.
"No, never, never!" said Miriam.
Little Brother shook his head, "*No!*"

但是住在那裏的國王，他的心腸很壞，
他對手下的人說：
    「把所有的小男嬰統統丟到河裏去！」
「喔，不行！不行！」媽媽說，把小摩西抱得更緊了。
「說什麼也不能讓人把我們的小寶寶扔到河裏去。」爸爸說。
「是啊，不行！絕對不行！」米利暗說。
小哥哥也搖著頭表示，「**不行！**」

"We'll hide our baby," said Mother.
But Baby Moses didn't like to be hidden away all day–
    he cried and cried.
Miriam was afraid the king's men would hear.
"Sh! Sh! Baby Moses," she whispered,
    but he cried the louder.
"Oh, what can we do?" asked Miriam.

「不如把小寶寶藏起來。」媽媽說。
但是小摩西不喜歡整天被藏著──
    他哭了又哭。
米利暗怕國王的手下會聽到哭聲，
「噓！噓！小寶貝。」她輕輕地在摩西耳邊說。
    但是他哭得更大聲了。
「噢！我們該怎麼辦才好？」米利暗問。

"We'll make a basket boat for Baby Moses
    and hide him in the rushes at the river's edge," said Mother.
They wove a tight little basket and painted it with pitch
    to keep it from leaking.
Mother put a soft pillow in it.
She laid Baby Moses on the soft pillow.

「我們不如用籃子為小摩西做一艘小船，
    把他藏在河邊的蘆葦叢裏。」媽媽說。
他們編織了一個牢固的籃子，再塗上厚厚的松香，
    避免籃子漏水。
媽媽在籃子裏放了一個軟軟的枕頭，
把小摩西放在柔軟的枕頭上。

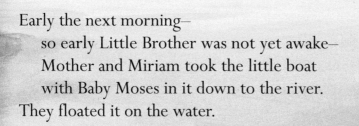

Early the next morning–
    so early Little Brother was not yet awake–
    Mother and Miriam took the little boat
    with Baby Moses in it down to the river.
They floated it on the water.

第二天一大早——
    摩西的小哥哥還沒睡醒——
    媽媽和米利暗就帶著籃子來到河邊，
    把小摩西連同小籃船放進河裏，
她們讓它漂浮在水面上。

Tall rushes kept the basket boat from floating away.
Mother left Miriam to watch while she went home and
    prayed God to keep her baby safe.
The sun shone warm.
The soft breezes blew.
The water rocked the little boat.
Baby Moses liked to be rocked.
He fell fast asleep.

13

長長的蘆葦保護著小籃船，不讓它被水沖走。
媽媽叫米利暗留下來，看著摩西，
　　自己回家禱告，祈求上帝讓她的小寶寶平安。
和煦的陽光照耀著大地，
輕柔的微風吹拂著水面。
小船在河裏盪漾。
小摩西喜歡搖呀搖，
他很快就睡著了。

Miriam hid in the bushes by the river.

She watched the basket boat as it rocked to and fro on the water.

But listen! Someone was coming.

Oh! Oh! Oh!

It was the king's daughter

    and her maids coming to bathe in the river.

Would she see the little boat?

Would *she* throw Baby Moses into the river?

米利暗躲在河邊的草叢中，
她看著小船在河水中來來回回搖晃著。
注意聽！有人來了。
喔！糟了！糟了！
原來是公主和她的侍女們，
　她們來到河邊沐浴。
她會看見那艘小船嗎？
她會把小摩西扔進河裏嗎？

16

The king's daughter came closer and closer.
She stopped at the river's edge and pointed to the little boat.
"Go," she said to her maid,
    "go bring the basket to me."
The king's daughter raised the cover.
"Oh, what a lovely baby!" she said.
"I want him for my very own."

公主越走越近。
她在河邊停住，指著那艘小船，
「去！」她對侍女說，
    「去把那個籃子拿過來給我。」
公主掀開蓋子。
「哦，多可愛的小嬰兒啊！」她說。
「我要收養他作我的孩子。」

Miriam came running.

She made a little bow to the king's daughter.

"Shall I get a nurse for the baby?"

"Yes," said the king's daughter, "go find a nurse
  to take care of the baby for me."

Miriam bowed again, and then she ran home as fast as she could go.

米利暗趕緊跑過來。

她向公主鞠躬請安，

「您要我為這小嬰兒找個褓姆嗎？」她問。

「好的。」公主回答說，「去找個褓姆來，
　幫我好好照顧這個小嬰兒。」

米利暗又鞠了一個躬，然後飛也似的跑回家去。

"Mother, Mother! Come, come!
The king's daughter found Baby Moses.
She wants a nurse for him.
She likes our baby.
She won't let anyone throw him into the river."

「媽媽，媽媽！快來啊，快來啊！
公主發現小摩西了。
她要我去找一個褓姆。
她喜歡我們的小寶貝，
她不會讓別人把他丟到河裏去了。」

Mother and Miriam hurried to the river.
There stood the king's daughter holding Baby Moses.
He was crying–he was afraid of the strange lady.
"Take this baby and nurse him for me;
    I will pay you wages," said the king's daughter.
Mother held out her arms for the baby.
Baby Moses smiled and held up his hands.
The king's daughter said to Mother,
    "Keep the baby for me until he is a big boy."

媽媽和米利暗急忙趕到河邊。
公主站在那裏，手裏抱著摩西。
摩西正在哇哇大哭——他害怕這個陌生的女人。
「把這個小嬰兒抱去，幫我好好照顧他；
    我會付你工錢，」公主說。
媽媽緊緊地抱住她的小寶貝。
嬰兒摩西笑了，還揮舞著他的雙手。
公主對媽媽說：
    「在他長大成為一個大男孩之前，你要一直照顧他。」

24

Mother took Baby Moses, and started up the path.
She was happy to be taking her baby home.
Now she wouldn't have to hide him any more.
Miriam was so happy she skipped and sang.
Baby Moses laughed and cooed.
He was happy too.
Father and Little Brother were waiting for them.
Little Brother jumped up and down and waved.

媽媽抱著小摩西上路了，
她很高興能帶著她的小寶貝回家。
以後再也不必把他藏起來了。
米利暗高興得又唱又跳。
小嬰兒摩西咯咯地笑，
他也很高興。
爸爸和小哥哥正等著他們回來。
小哥哥開心地跳上跳下，手舞足蹈。

26

When all were safely in their home again,
    they all kneeled in prayer around Baby Moses' cradle—
Father, Mother, Miriam, and Little Brother.
"Thank You, God," prayed Father,
    "Thank You for keeping our baby safe."

他們平安回到家之後，
    大家一同圍著小摩西的搖籃禱告——
爸爸、媽媽、米利暗和小哥哥。
「上帝，謝謝你，」爸爸說，
    「謝謝你保守我們的小寶貝平安。」

29

小小嬰孩耶穌
Baby Jesus

可愛的小耶穌快要誕生了，
可是媽媽馬利亞還沒找到住宿的地方，
最後他們只找到一間又舊又小的馬廄……

Clip–clop–clip–clop,
    went Small Donkey's hoofs
    as he s-l-o-w-l-y climbed the last hill.
Mary rode on Small Donkey's back.
Joseph walked by Small Donkey's side.
Mary and Joseph were very, very tired.
Small Donkey was tired, too.
They had come a long, long way.
From the top of the hill, O happy sight, they saw the lights of Bethlehem!

踢——踏——踢——踏，
　　小驢子的蹄子一步一步地走得好慢，
　　牠慢慢地爬上最後一座山。
馬利亞騎在小驢子的背上，
約瑟走在小驢子身邊。
馬利亞和約瑟覺得好累好累，
小驢子也好累好累。
他們已經走了一段漫長的路。
從山頂往下看，喔，多麼令人開心的景色，
他們終於看到了伯利恆的燈光！

Joseph walked faster now.

Clip–clop, clip–clop, clip–clop, hurried Small Donkey,
down the hill, through the gate, into the little town,
where they would rest and sleep.

At the inn, Joseph asked for a room.

"We have no room," said the innkeeper.

"Is there no place where we can sleep?" asked Joseph.

"Only in the stable……I am sorry."

約瑟開始加快腳步。

踢——踏——踢——踏——踢——踏，小驢子也加快步伐，
　　他們從山頂走下去，穿過城門，來到了一座小城鎮，
　　他們要在這裏休息過夜。

在小客棧裏，約瑟詢問是否有空房。

「我們沒有空房了。」客棧主人說。

「沒有地方能讓我們過夜嗎？」約瑟問。

「只剩下馬廄了……真是不好意思。」

34

Joseph led Small Donkey toward the stable.
He opened the creaky old door.
He held up the lantern the innkeeper gave him,
    and looked around inside.
He saw Spotted Cow, and Woolly Lamb,
    and stalls that were empty.
In one empty stall he tied Small Donkey.
In another he made a bed of straw for Mary and himself.
Soon they were fast asleep.

約瑟牽著小驢子走到馬廄。
他推開那扇破舊的門，
手裏提著客棧主人給他的油燈，
    往四處看了一下。
他看到花斑牛和茸毛羊，
    和一些空的馬廄房間。
他把小驢子綁在一間空的馬房裏。
再到另外一間房間裏，
用稻草為馬利亞和他自己鋪了一張床。
他們很快就都睡著了。

During the night the most wonderful thing happened—
Baby Jesus was born!
Joseph filled a manger with clean new hay.
Mary wrapped the baby in soft white cloth,
    and laid Him in the manger.
The animals seemed pleased about Baby Jesus.
Spotted Cow mooed softly,
    Woolly Lamb tinkled his bell,
    and Small Donkey looked and looked.

37

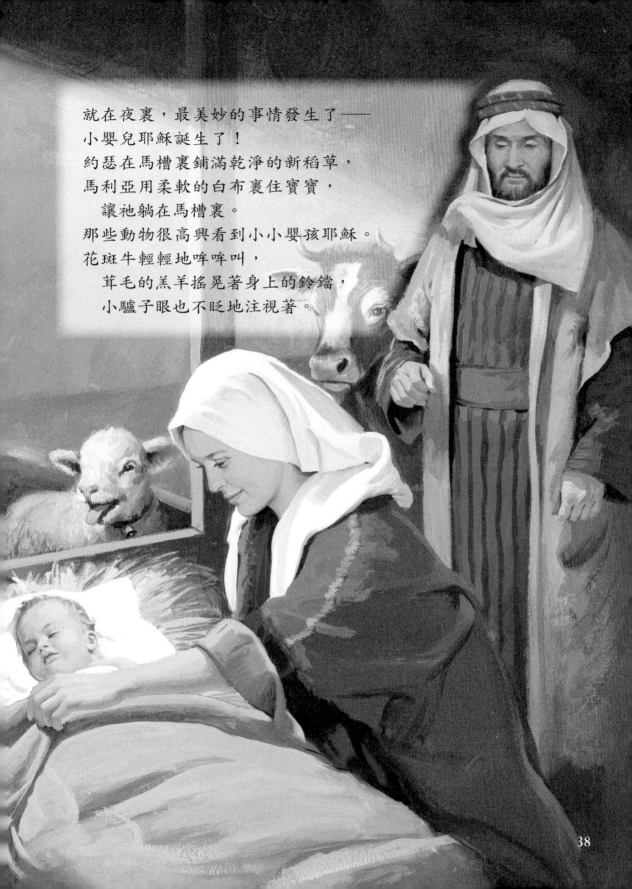

就在夜裏，最美妙的事情發生了——
小嬰兒耶穌誕生了！
約瑟在馬槽裏鋪滿乾淨的新稻草，
馬利亞用柔軟的白布裹住寶寶，
　　讓祂躺在馬槽裏。
那些動物很高興看到小小嬰孩耶穌。
花斑牛輕輕地哞哞叫，
　　茸毛的羔羊搖晃著身上的鈴鐺，
　　小驢子眼也不眨地注視著。

That night, in a field near the little town,
    shepherds were guarding their sheep.
Suddenly a bright light, as bright as the sun,
    shone all around them.
The shepherds were afraid and covered their faces.
The sheep were afraid and huddled together.

那天夜晚，在小鎮附近的原野上，
　　有一群牧羊人正看守著他們的羊。
突然間，一道亮光，
　　就像陽光一樣照亮他們的四周。
牧羊人害怕地遮住他們的臉。
羊群也害怕地緊靠在一起。

"Don't be afraid," said a kind, gentle voice.
The shepherds uncovered their faces.
They saw an angel, all glowing with light.
Said the angel, "I bring you good tidings of great joy!
Jesus, your Saviour, is born.
You will find Him lying in a manger."
Then the sky was filled with shining angels singing the glory song—
  "Glory to God it the highest, and on earth peace,
      good will toward men."

「不要害怕！」一個親切溫柔的聲音說。
牧羊人放下掩面的手，
他們看見天使，他的全身充滿著榮光。
天使說：「我為你們帶來了大喜樂的好消息！
耶穌，你們的救世主，已誕生了。
你們會看見祂躺臥在一個馬槽裏。」
接著，天空中出現好多明亮的天使，他們唱著榮耀的歌——
「在至高之處榮耀歸與神，
　在地上平安歸與祂所喜悅的人。」

As the angels went farther and farther away,
they looked like a twinkling bright star
in the dark night sky above Bethlehem.
"Come," said the shepherds, "let us go see."
They ran all the way to the stable,
and there they found Joseph and Mary and
Baby Jesus in His manger bed.

天使們漸漸遠去，
　　他們看起來就像黑夜裏一顆閃亮的大星星，
　　高掛在伯利恆黑暗的夜空中。
「走！」牧羊人說，「我們一起去看看！」
他們朝著馬廄一路跑去，
　　就在那裏，他們找到約瑟和馬利亞，
　　還有躺臥在馬槽裏的小小嬰孩耶穌。

44

In a faraway country, Wise Men saw the angel star.
They said, "It is the star of the Baby King.
Let us go worship Him, and take Him presents."
The Wise Men made ready their gifts.
One Wise Man filled a bag with gold.
Another filled a jar with frankincense,
    the perfume of flowers.
And another filled a special box with myrrh,
    the perfume of spices.

在一個遙遠的國家，有博士看見了那顆天使星星。
他們說：「那顆星就是新生之王的星星。
我們去敬拜祂，獻禮物給祂！」
博士準備好他們的禮物。
一位博士裝了一袋金子，
另一位博士裝了一罐乳香，
　　那是花朵的香味。
最後一位博士準備一個特別的盒子，
　　盒子裏裝滿了芬芳的沒藥。

The Wise Men gathered up their gifts,
    mounted their camels, and rode toward the star.
They crossed rivers and hills and sandy deserts—
    sometimes it was hot,
    sometimes it was cold,
    but always rode on, following the star.

博士們將禮物準備好了，
　　就騎上駱駝，朝著星星的方向出發。
他們穿越了河流、山丘和沙漠──
　　有時天氣很熱，
　　有時天氣很冷，
　　但是他們仍然跟著那顆星星，不斷地前進。

49

Then one evening the star stopped above a house
    in the little town of Bethlehem.
The Wise Men made their camels kneel
    in front of the house.
They climbed off the camels' humped backs, and taking their gifts,
    they knocked on the door.

一天晚上，那顆星星停在一間房子上方，
    那房子是在伯利恆的小鎮上。
博士們叫駱駝在房子前跪下守候。
他們從駱駝的背上下來，拿著禮物，
    上前去敲門。

Joseph opened the door–
    and there inside was Mary
    holding Baby Jesus.
The Wise Men bowed with their
    faces to the floor and worshiped
    the baby they called king.
They gave Him their gifts–
    the bag of gold,
    the jar of frankincense,
    the special box of myrrh.
Then the Wise Men said good-bye,
    mounted their camels,
    and began their long
        journey home.

約瑟打開門——
    馬利亞坐在裏面，
    抱著小耶穌。
博士們臉伏於地，
    跪拜這位將來要作王的嬰孩。
他們把禮物獻給祂——
    一袋金子，
    一罐乳香，
    一盒特別的沒藥。
博士們跟他們道別，
    騎上駱駝，
    踏上了他們漫長的
    回家旅程。

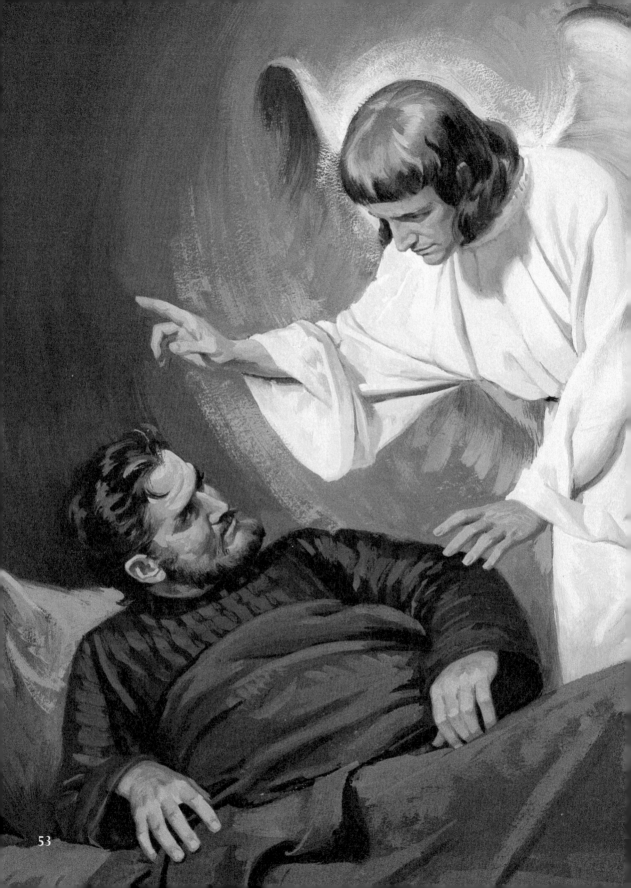

53

One dark night when Joseph was asleep, and Mary was asleep,
    and Baby Jesus was asleep, an angel whispered to Joseph.
"Get up quickly," he said. "Take Mary and the Baby and flee
    into Egypt. The wicked king is trying to find the Baby to
    do Him harm. Stay in Egypt until I tell you it is safe to return."
The king was angry because the people were saying
    that some day Baby Jesus would be king.

在一個黑夜裏，約瑟睡著了，馬利亞睡著了，
    小嬰兒耶穌也睡著了，一位天使輕聲對約瑟說話。
「快起來！」他說。「帶著馬利亞和小嬰孩逃到埃及去。
    邪惡的國王正在尋找小耶穌，想要殺害祂。」
    你們要待在埃及，直到我告訴你們安全了，你們再回來。」
國王很生氣，因為人們都在傳說，
    有一天小嬰兒耶穌將成為國王。

54

Joseph got up quickly.

He told Mary what the angel had said.

He went to the stable for Small Donkey.

Mary wrapped Baby Jesus snug and warm.

Joseph helped Mary on Small Donkey's back.

He handed her Baby Jesus.

Clip-clop, clip-clop, went Small Donkey's hoofs as they went out
through Bethlehem's gate,
and turned down the road
toward Egypt.

The wicked king
couldn't find
Baby Jesus now.

約瑟急忙起身。

他把天使的話告訴馬利亞，

並去馬廄牽小驢子，

馬利亞把小嬰兒耶穌包得既舒適又溫暖，

約瑟扶馬利亞騎上驢子之後，

把小嬰兒耶穌交給她。

踢—踏—踢—踏，隨著小驢子的蹄聲漸漸遠去，

　　他們出了伯利恆的城門，

　　朝著埃及出發。

那位壞國王就無法找到小耶穌了。

Joseph and Mary, Baby Jesus,
　　and Small Donkey lived in Egypt a long time.
Baby Jesus learned to walk and to talk.
Then on night the angel again whispered to Joseph,
　　"The wicked king is dead. It is safe to go home."
Once more Mary rode on Small Donkey's back,
　　but the Boy Jesus didn't ride all the way now.
Sometimes He walked and helped to lead Small Donkey.
They didn't go to Bethlehem where Jesus was born.
They went to Nazareth, Joseph and Mary's old home.

約瑟、馬利亞、小耶穌，
　　和小驢子在埃及住了很久的時間。
小耶穌已經學會走路和講話了。
一天晚上，天使又輕聲對約瑟說：
　　「壞國王死了，你們現在可以安全回家去了。」
再一次地，馬利亞又騎上驢子，
　　但這次小耶穌並沒有一路上都騎著驢子。
有時候祂會自己走路，手裏牽著驢，領著牠的方向。
他們沒有回到耶穌的出生地伯利恆城，
反而去了約瑟和馬利亞的老家拿撒勒城。

Joseph and Mary were glad to be back in their old home.
Small Donkey was glad to be back in his own stable.
When Mary tucked the Boy Jesus into His own bed,
     she told Him good-night stories.
She told about—
     Baby Moses and his basket boat,
     about when the angels sang the glory song,
     about the Wise Men followed the star,
     and worshiped the Baby as their king.

約瑟和馬利亞很高興能回到他們的老家。
　　驢子也很高興能回到牠自己的舊馬廄。
馬利亞把耶穌放到祂自己的床上，
　　講睡前故事給祂聽。
她說到——
　　小小嬰孩摩西和他的籃子小船，
　　天使的美妙歌聲，
　　還有博士們跟著星星走，
　　向小耶穌國王朝拜。

約瑟
和他的哥哥們
Joseph and His Brothers

約瑟很開心地把他的新衣服穿給哥哥們看，
可是十個哥哥卻生氣了，
因為他們嫉妒約瑟有新的彩衣，
哥哥們打算把約瑟賣了……

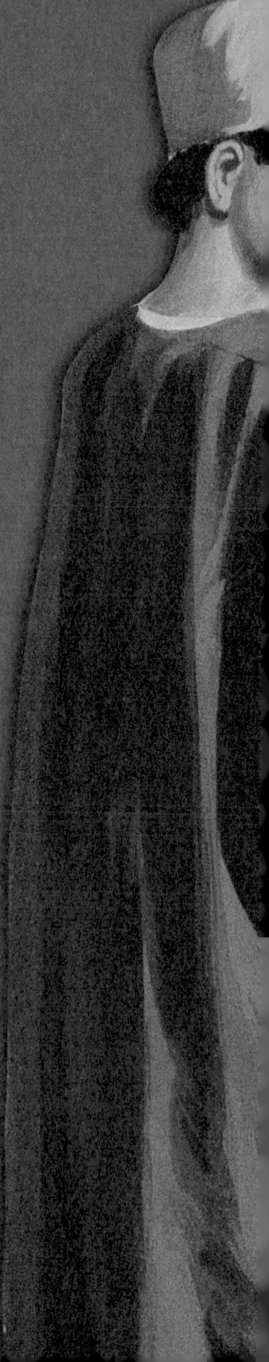

Joseph showed his new coat of many colors
    to his ten older brothers.
They said,
    "Our father never made us coats of many colors."
The brothers were angry, very angry,
    because of Joseph's new coat.

約瑟開心地把他彩色的新袍子
　　穿給十位哥哥看。
他們說：
　　「爸爸從來沒有為我們織過彩色的外袍。」
哥哥們生氣了，他們非常生氣，
　　因為約瑟的新袍子。

One night while Joseph lay sleeping he dreamed a dream—a strange dream.
He dreamed he and his brothers were in the field tying sheaves of wheat.
Suddenly his sheaf stood up straight and tall.
His brothers' sheaves gathered around and bowed to his sheaf.
　　Joseph told his brothers the strange dream.
They said, "Do you think we are going to bow down to you?"
The brothers were angry, very angry,
　　because of Joseph's strange dream.

一天夜裏，約瑟做了一個夢——個奇怪的夢。
他夢見他和哥哥們在田裏收麥子，綁禾捆。
突然間，他的禾捆站了起來，又高又挺。
哥哥們的禾捆卻圍了過來，朝他的禾捆下拜。
　　約瑟把這個奇怪的夢告訴哥哥們。
他們說：「你以為我們會向你下拜嗎？」
哥哥們生氣了，他們非常生氣，
　　因為約瑟這個奇怪的夢。

One day, Joseph's brothers went to a faraway place
    to find green grass for the sheep.
When they had been gone a long time,
    father Jacob said to Joseph,
    "Go see if your brothers are well,
    and if it be well with the sheep."
Joseph put on his coat of many colors.
He said good-by to his father.
He said good-by to his little brother Benjamin.
Then he began the long, long walk.

一天，哥哥們去了很遠的地方，
    為要尋找一塊能夠牧羊的草地。
他們去了好久，都還沒回來，
    爸爸雅各對約瑟說：
    「去看看你的哥哥們是不是還好，
    羊群是不是也都還好。」
約瑟穿上彩色的袍子。
向爸爸道別，
也向弟弟便雅憫道別，
接著，他就踏上了漫長的路程。

Joseph walked, and walked, and walked. At last, from the top of a hill,
  he saw his brothers and the sheep
  camped by the road that leads to Egypt.
Joseph shouted to them.
He waved to them. He was happy to see them.

約瑟一路走著，走著。最後，他終於從山頂上，
  看見他的哥哥們和羊群，
  在通往埃及的路旁紮營。
約瑟向他們大聲喊叫，
並向他們揮手。他好高興能見到他們。

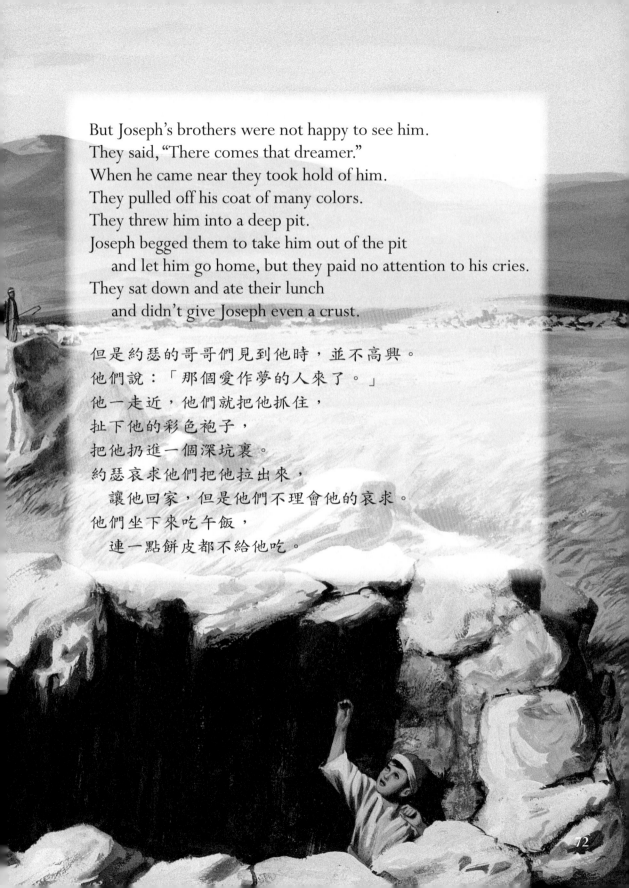

But Joseph's brothers were not happy to see him.
They said, "There comes that dreamer."
When he came near they took hold of him.
They pulled off his coat of many colors.
They threw him into a deep pit.
Joseph begged them to take him out of the pit
    and let him go home, but they paid no attention to his cries.
They sat down and ate their lunch
    and didn't give Joseph even a crust.

但是約瑟的哥哥們見到他時，並不高興。
他們說：「那個愛作夢的人來了。」
他一走近，他們就把他抓住，
扯下他的彩色袍子，
把他扔進一個深坑裏。
約瑟哀求他們把他拉出來，
    讓他回家，但是他們不理會他的哀求。
他們坐下來吃午飯，
    連一點餅皮都不給他吃。

Down the dusty road that leads to Egypt came traders with their camels.
Said the brothers,
     "Let's sell Joseph to the traders."
So they took Joseph up out of the pit
     and sold him for twenty pieces of silver.

在通往埃及的泥濘路上，來了一群駱駝商隊。
那些兄弟們彼此說：
     「我們把約瑟賣給商人吧！」
於是他們將約瑟從坑裏拉出來，
     以二十塊銀幣的價格賣給了商人。

The traders took Joseph and went on their way.
From the road, Joseph could see the hill
    Where his father's tent was pitched.
He knew Benjamin was there with his father.
If only he could be there too. Joseph cried, and cried, and cried.
Then Joseph stopped crying.
He said, "I will be brave. God will take care of me."

商人們帶著約瑟繼續上路。
一路上，約瑟可以看見那座山，
　　就是他爸爸紮營的那座山。
他知道便雅憫和爸爸就在那裏。
如果他也能在那裏該有多好。約瑟哭了，他一直哭，哭了又哭。
最後，約瑟不哭了。
他說：「我一定要勇敢！因為上帝會照顧我。」

Down in Egypt the traders sold Joseph
   to a man named Potiphar.
Joseph had to work hard.
His legs got tired, his back got tired,
   but he did his work well.
When he swept the floor he was careful
   to sweep in the corners.
When he pulled weeds in the garden
   he pulled every one.
Potiphar said, "You are a good worker, Joseph."

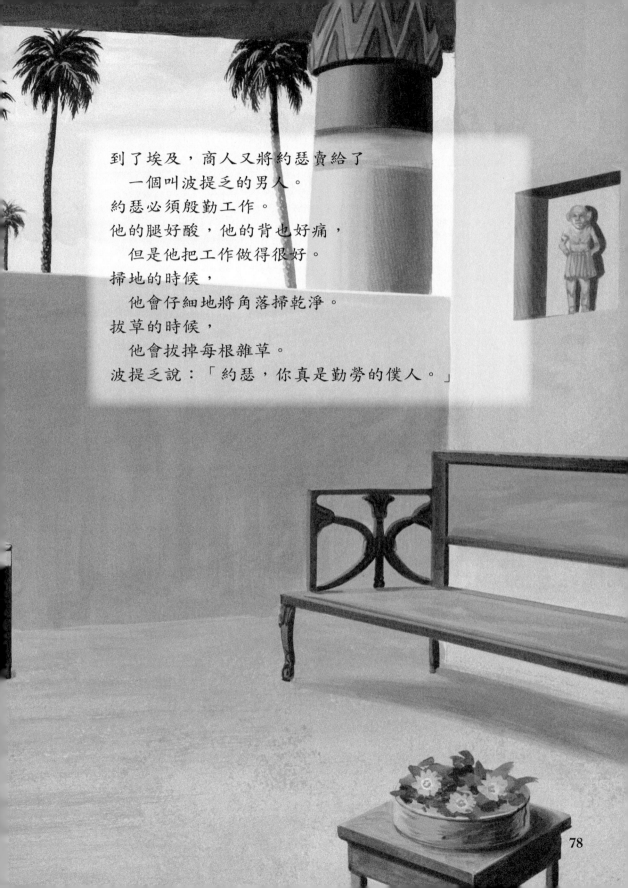

到了埃及，商人又將約瑟賣給了
　　一個叫波提乏的男人。
約瑟必須殷勤工作。
他的腿好酸，他的背也好痛，
　　但是他把工作做得很好。
掃地的時候，
　　他會仔細地將角落掃乾淨。
拔草的時候，
　　他會拔掉每根雜草。
波提乏說：「約瑟，你真是勤勞的僕人。」

Joseph learned to talk like the people of Egypt.
He wore clothes like the people of Egypt.
He cut his hair like the people of Egypt.
But there was one thing he would never,
    never do like the people of Egypt.
The people of Egypt prayed to an idol,
    or to a cat, and sometimes even to a frog.
But Joseph prayed always to the God of heaven,
    as Jacob his father had taught him.

約瑟學會像埃及人一樣講話。
他的穿著也像埃及人。
他連頭髮都剪得像埃及人。
但是有一件事，是他永遠永遠
　　都不會像埃及人那樣做的。
埃及人會向偶像祈禱，
　　他們也會向貓，甚至有時候會向青蛙祈禱。
約瑟只對天上的上帝禱告，
　　那是他的爸爸雅各教導他的。

Many many years went by.
Joseph grew to be a very wise man.
Now it happened that the king of Egypt
    wanted a very wise man to build storehouses
    and to fill the storehouses with corn.

The king said,
    "Where could I find a man wiser than Joseph?
    I will get Joseph to build the storehouses.
    I will have Joseph fill them with corn."

過了好幾年。

約瑟長大了，成為一位很聰明的年輕人。

埃及的國王此時正好需要一個有智慧的人，

　來蓋倉房，儲存穀糧。

國王說：

　「我到哪裏可以找到比約瑟更聰明的人呢？

　我要叫約瑟來建造倉房。

　我要叫他把倉房裝滿穀糧。」

So the king made Joseph ruler of Egypt
  next to himself.
He said to the people of Egypt,
  "Whatever Joseph says, you must do."
Joseph rode in a shiny chariot.
He drove a team of prancing horses.
Joseph built the storehouses for the king.
He filled the storehouses with corn.

國王任命約瑟為宰相，
　地位僅次於他。
他昭告埃及的全國百姓，說：
　「不論約瑟說什麼，你們都必須照做。」
約瑟站在閃閃發光的雙輪馬車上，
指揮著精神抖擻的馬車隊伍。
約瑟為國王建造了許多倉房，
倉房裏都儲滿了穀糧。

Then came the time of no rain.
And because there was no rain, nothing grew.
There was no corn for the people to eat,
    no corn for the cows or the horses.
The people cried to the king,
    "Give us corn or we die."
The king said, "Go to Joseph—he will help you."
Joseph opened up the storehouses and sold the people corn.

乾旱無雨的日子來了。
天空不降雨，所以什麼東西也長不出來。
人民沒有食物可吃，
　牛或馬也沒有糧草可吃。
人民向國王哭求：
　「給我們糧食吃，不然我們就要餓死了。」
國王說：「去找約瑟——他會幫助你們。」
約瑟打開倉房，將裏面的穀糧賣給人民。

86

One day Joseph saw ten little donkeys with empty sacks on
  their backs coming toward the storehouse
  where he was selling corn. Beside the ten little donkeys
  walked his ten older brothers.
The brothers didn't know Joseph, but Joseph knew them.
They bowed to Joseph with their faces to the ground.
Joseph remembered his dream about the sheaves.

有一天，約瑟看見十隻小驢子背著空麻袋，
  朝著他賣穀糧的倉房走過來。
    走在這十隻驢子旁邊的，
      就是他的十個哥哥。
哥哥們已認不出約瑟了，但約瑟還認得他們。
他們臉伏於地，向約瑟下拜。
約瑟想起了那個關於禾捆的夢。

Joseph talked with his brothers,
　　but he didn't tell them
　　who he was–not yet.
"Is your father well?" asked Joseph.
"Do you have another brother?"
"Our father is well," they said.
"We have a younger brother at home."
"When you come again to buy corn," said Joseph,
　　"bring your younger brother with you."
Joseph filled their empty sacks with corn,
　　and the ten little donkeys went home.

約瑟和他的哥哥們說話，
　　但是他沒有告訴他們他是誰——
　　時候還沒有到。
「你們的爸爸好嗎？」約瑟問，
「你們還有兄弟嗎？」
「我們的爸爸很好。」他們說，
「我們還有一個弟弟在家裏。」
「下次你們再來買糧食的時候，」約瑟說，
　　「把你們的弟弟也帶來。」
約瑟將他們的麻袋裝滿了穀糧，
　　然後十隻小驢子就啟程回家了。

The brothers came again to buy corn.
This time Benjamin was with them.
Joseph stood up before his brothers,
    and they still did not know him.
Then he said, "I am Joseph."
Benjamin was happy to see Joseph,
    but the ten older brothers were afraid.
They said, "Now Joseph will punish us for selling him to the traders."
But Joseph said, "Don't be afraid. Come to me."
Joseph hugged Benjamin and all his brothers.

哥哥們又來買糧食了，
這次弟弟便雅憫也一起來了。
約瑟站在他的哥哥們面前，
　　他們仍然認不出他是誰。
他說：「我是約瑟。」
便雅憫很高興見到約瑟，
　　但是十位哥哥卻很害怕。
他們說：「約瑟一定會懲罰我們，因為當初我們把他賣給商人。」
但是約瑟說：「不要害怕，到我這裏來！」
他擁抱便雅憫和十個哥哥。

Joseph's brothers were now good, kind men.
They were sorry for what they had done.
Joseph gave each of them a new coat.
He sent home with his brothers many presents for Jacob, his father.
He sent wagons to move them all down to Egypt,
    where there was plenty of corn.

約瑟的哥哥們後來都成了仁慈的好人。
他們對以前所做的事很後悔。
約瑟給他們每人一件新袍子。
他叫哥哥們帶好多禮物回去，送給爸爸，
又派了許多馬車把他們全都接到埃及來住，
    因為埃及有足夠的糧食。

94

Joseph watched the road—
    and one day he saw the wagons he had sent,
    and the ten little donkeys, and his brothers with his father's sheep,
    all coming down the road to Egypt.
Joseph jumped into his chariot.
He galloped his horses up the road to meet them.

約瑟望著遠方的路——
　　有一天，他終於看見他派去的馬車，
　　以及十隻小驢子和他的兄弟們，還有爸爸的羊群，
　　朝著埃及前來。
約瑟跳上他的馬車，
快馬加鞭地奔向他們。

When Jacob saw Joseph coming he climbed down from the wagon.
Joseph jumped down from his chariot.
He ran to his father and threw his arms around him.
He hugged him, and hugged him!
Now, Joseph and his father and Benjamin and his ten older brothers
would all live together happily in the land of Egypt.

雅各看見約瑟過來，他趕緊下了馬車。
約瑟也跳下馬車，
奔向他的爸爸，並且伸出雙臂。
他抱住爸爸雅各，緊緊地抱住！
約瑟、爸爸、便雅憫和十個哥哥，
　　終於可以在埃及這個地方一起快樂的生活了。

耶穌和暴風雨
Jesus and the Storm

突然，海面上刮起了狂風暴雨。
巨浪把他們的船拋來拋去，上下搖晃。
眼看著船就要沉了，大家呼求著耶穌……

Jesus stood in a boat—a fishing boat with oars and a sail—
and talked to the many people
who had come to hear Him.
All day long Jesus told them stories.
When it was evening Jesus said to His helpers,
"Let us cross over to the other side of the lake and rest."

耶穌站在一艘有槳有帆的漁船上——
　　向許多來聽故事的人講話。
耶穌一整天都對他們講故事。
到了傍晚，耶穌向祂的助手說：
「我們把船划到湖的對岸去歇一歇吧！」

103

Berran

Jesus' helpers untied the boat.
They pushed it from the shore and raised the sail.
One man sat in the back of the boat
    to guide it with the steering tiller.
The boat moved slowly at first, and then faster
    across the quiet blue water.

耶穌的助手解開了船的繩索，
把船推離岸邊，然後拉起船帆。
一名門徒坐在船的後方，
    掌控著船舵，引導船前進。
船剛開始慢慢地移動，然後漸漸地加快速度，
    越過一片寂靜的藍色湖水。

A round yellow moon came up over the lake.
The stars twinkled high overhead.
Jesus was so very tired, He lay down
    with His head on a pillow
    and was soon sound asleep.
The man at the back steered carefully.
The boat sailed on and on and on.

金黃色的一輪明月在湖面上升起。
繁星在高高的天空中閃爍。
耶穌非常疲累，
    祂靠著枕頭躺了下來，
    很快地，祂就酣然入睡了。
門徒在船的後方小心掌舵。
船持續地向前航行。

Berron

Suddenly a fierce wind began to blow.
It blew a black cloud over the moon.
It blew black clouds over the stars.
It whipped the water into huge angry waves.
The waves tossed the boat this way,
and that way, and up and down.
There was lightning!
There was thunder!

突然間，刮起一陣強風，
強風吹動烏雲，遮蔽了月亮，
也遮掩了星星，
還掀起了狂怒巨浪。
巨浪把船一下拋向這邊，一下拋向那邊，
然後上上下下地搖晃，
接著一陣閃電！
還有隆隆雷聲！

The man at the tiller tried to steer the boat, but he couldn't.
Other men tried to row the boat with oars, but they couldn't.
Water filled the boat. It began to sink.
The men were afraid. They woke Jesus—
"Lord save us; we perish!" they cried.

掌舵的人想駕好這艘船，可是他辦不到。

其他人拼命想划好這艘船，可是他們無能為力。

船身進水了，它開始下沉。

大家都很害怕，他們叫醒耶穌——

「主啊，救救我們；我們快要沒命啦！」他們哭喊著。

Jesus heard their cry for help.
He felt the angry wind.
He saw the lightning flash.
He heard the noisy thunder.
But He was not afraid.
He stood up and said to the wind and waves,
　　"Peace-be still."

耶穌聽到他們的求助聲。
祂感覺到狂風在怒吼。
祂看到閃電照亮了天空。
祂聽到隆隆的雷聲。
但是祂一點都不害怕。
祂站起來吩咐風和浪：
　　「平了吧！靜了吧！」

Berran

The wind stopped blowing. The waves were still.
The clouds went away, and the stars twinkled again.
The boat sailed on the sparkling path
   that the moon made on the water,
   and crossed to the other side of the lake.
"Why were you afraid?" Jesus asked His helpers.
"Why were you afraid when I was with you?"

風平了，浪也靜了。
烏雲消散之後，繁星再度閃爍。
船在月光照耀下的閃亮水道航行，
　駛向湖的對岸。
「你們為何害怕呢？」耶穌問祂的助手。
「我既然與你們同在，你們為什麼還害怕呢？」

Jesus says to boys and girls today—
  "Don't be afraid when the lightning flashes,
  and the thunder crashes,
  and the strong winds blow."
"I am with you always," says Jesus,
  "in the dark and in the storm,
  I will never leave you. Don't be afraid."

耶穌也告訴今日的小朋友——
  「不要害怕，即使有閃電強光，
  雷聲隆隆，或是強風呼嘯，」
「我永遠與你們同在。」耶穌說。
  「無論天有多黑，風雨有多大，
  我都不會離開你們。你們不要害怕！」

116

小小嬰孩摩西
Baby Moses

1 小朋友，故事中的米利暗在你心中是怎樣的一個姐姐呢？

2 小嬰孩摩西一出生就遇到生命危險，是誰幫助他度過危險的？

3 你有哪些家人？你們是不是也和摩西的家人一樣彼此相愛呢？

4 摩西的家人遇到害怕困難的事情時，他們向誰求助呢？

5 小朋友，你感到害怕、危險或困難的時候，你可以向誰求助呢？

小小嬰孩耶穌
Baby Jesus

1 小朋友，你覺得誕生在馬槽的耶穌，或出生在皇宮的耶穌，哪一個是你比較容易親近的？為什麼？

2 小小嬰孩耶穌與摩西一樣，一出生就有生命危險，幫助耶穌脫離危險的有哪些人呢？說說看這些人是怎麼做到的？

3 小小嬰孩摩西和耶穌都因為家人的疼愛而脫離生命危險，你覺得家人可以幫助你解決生活上的什麼問題呢？趕快告訴家人你的問題吧！

約瑟和他的哥哥們
Joseph and His Brothers

① 小朋友，你覺得約瑟在十個哥哥面前的表現，是不是有討他們的喜歡？

② 你認為約瑟在生活中有沒有對哥哥們恭敬呢？

③ 哥哥們喜歡約瑟嗎？喜歡與否都請你說出幾個你的理由。

④ 一個在班上表現很受歡迎的優秀同學，你覺得他有哪些可能受歡迎的理由？

⑤ 有什麼原因，會讓一個班上優秀的學生不受同學歡迎呢？

⑥ 你在班上或家裏受歡迎嗎？為什麼？

耶穌和暴風雨
Jesus and the Storm

① 耶穌的助手掌舵著漁船，忽然遇到暴風雨，他們在懼怕中怎麼度過的？

② 在暴風雨的夜晚，突然停電，你獨自一個人在家，感到非常恐懼，但你可以怎麼做？

③ 耶穌告訴助手，只要有祂同在船上就不用害怕，耶穌為什麼這樣說？

④ 小朋友，你在生活中遇到害怕的事時，耶穌要與你同在，你願意讓耶穌住在你心中嗎？

耶穌和孩子們
Jesus and the Children

孩子們高興地一路跟隨耶穌來到聖殿，
卻看到殿裏的商人不斷吆喝、數錢。
耶穌生氣了，祂把那些商人統統趕走……

120

Mark and Sara were waiting with
　　Mother and baby Esther to see Jesus.
Other children were waiting with their mothers.
Jesus' helpers frowned at them—
"Can't you see that Jesus is busy?
He has no time for children."

馬可和撒拉，還有媽媽和嬰兒以斯帖，
　正等著要見耶穌。
其他的孩子也和他們的媽媽一起等待著。
耶穌的助手對他們皺起眉頭——
「你們沒看到耶穌正在忙嗎？
祂沒有時間理會你們這些小孩子。」

122

Mark and Sara, and Mother with baby
   Esther turned slowly away.
Mark hung his head, and watched
   the dust of the path squish up
   between his brown toes.
Sara looked back at Jesus.
A tear ran down her cheek.

123

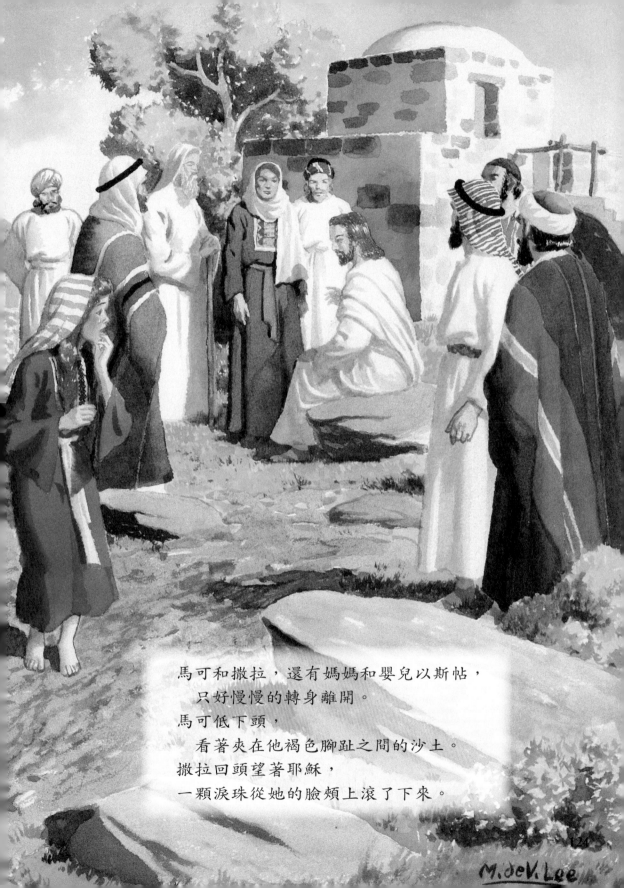

馬可和撒拉，還有媽媽和嬰兒以斯帖，
　　只好慢慢的轉身離開。
馬可低下頭，
　　看著夾在他褐色腳趾之間的沙土。
撒拉回頭望著耶穌，
一顆淚珠從她的臉頰上滾了下來。

124

M.deV.Lee

Then they heard Jesus say to His helpers,
  "Suffer the little children to come unto me,
    and forbid them not."
All the children ran to Jesus.
Jesus took baby Esther on His lap.
He smiled and touched Sara's cheek where the tear had run down.
He put His hand on Mark's head.
The children took turns standing close to Jesus.
He told them stories.

那時，他們聽見耶穌對助手說：
「讓那些小孩到我這裏來，
不要禁止他們！」
於是，所有的小孩都跑向耶穌。
耶穌將嬰兒以斯帖抱在祂的腿上。
祂含笑地撫摸撒拉流過淚水的臉頰，
祂摸摸馬可的頭。
孩子們輪流地站在耶穌旁邊，
祂說故事給他們聽。

On the way home Mark whistled a happy tune.
Sara skipped ahead, and then she waited
    and took Mother's hand.
"I wish we could see Jesus every day," she said.
"Maybe," said Mother,
    "maybe soon Jesus will come to the Temple."

在回家的路上，馬可吹著快樂的口哨。
撒拉走在前面又蹦又跳，她停下來等媽媽，
    並握住媽媽的手。
「我真希望每天都能見到耶穌。」她說。
「也許，」媽媽回答，
    「也許耶穌很快就會來聖殿了。」

MacV.Lee

One day Mark and Sara heard people singing the hosanna song.
They ran to see why the people were singing.
They saw Jesus riding on a colt coming down the road.
People were laying their coats on the road for Him to ride over.
Boys were waving palm branches and shouting.
Girls were tossing flowers and singing.

有一天，馬可和撒拉聽見大家高唱讚頌歌《和散那》。
他們跑去看大家為什麼在唱歌。
他們看見耶穌騎著驢子沿路過來。
大家把外衣鋪在地上，讓祂騎著驢在他們的衣服上經過。
男孩子揮舞著棕櫚樹枝，並高聲呼喊。
女孩子一邊撒花，一邊唱歌。

"May we go with Jesus?" asked Mark. "May we?" said Sara.
Mark's father cut a palm branch for him,
   and Mother helped Sara fill a basket with flowers.
Mark waved his palm branch and shouted,
   "Hosanna to the Son of David, Hosanna, Hosanna!"
Sara tossed flowers on the road and sang, *"Hosanna, Hosanna."*
It was like a big parade.
It made Jesus happy to hear the children shout and sing.

「我們可以跟耶穌一起去嗎？」馬可問。「可以嗎？」撒拉也問。
馬可的爸爸為馬可砍下一根棕櫚樹枝，
   撒拉的媽媽幫撒拉裝滿一籃子的花。
馬可揮舞著他的棕櫚樹枝，高聲呼喊：
   「和散那歸於大衛的子孫，和散那！和散那！」
撒拉將花朵撒在路上，唱著：「和散那，和散那。」
它就像是一場盛大的遊行。
耶穌很高興聽到孩子們的歡呼聲和歌唱聲。

132

M. deV. Lee

The parade came to the top of a hill.
Jesus stopped the colt, and looked down over the hill.
The boys stopped waving their palm branches and looked.
The girls stopped tossing flowers and looked.
All the people stopped and looked down over the hill.
What did they see down over the hill?

遊行隊伍來到山頂。
耶穌停下驢駒，注視著山下。
男孩子停止揮舞樹枝，一起注視山下。
女孩子停止拋撒花朵，也一起注視山下。
所有人都停下來注視山下。
他們到底在看山腳下的什麼景色呢？

133
M.deV.Lee

There was a brook down over the hill,
    a sing–along, laugh-along brook,
    but they were not looking at the brook.
There was a city with a high stone wall down over the hill,
    but they were not looking
    at the city with the high stone wall.

山下有一條小溪，
    潺潺流水聲，好像在吟唱歡笑，
    但是他們並不是在看這條小溪。
山腳下有一座圍著高牆的石頭城，
    但是他們也不是在看那座圍著高牆的石頭城。

137

M. deV. Lee

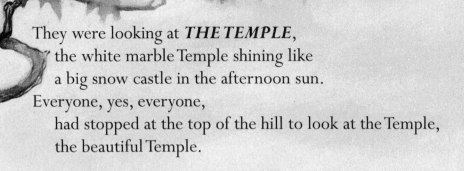

They were looking at **THE TEMPLE**,
 the white marble Temple shining like
 a big snow castle in the afternoon sun.
Everyone, yes, everyone,
 had stopped at the top of the hill to look at the Temple,
 the beautiful Temple.

他們看的是那座聖殿，
　　那座有著白色大理石的聖殿，
　　在午後的陽光下，閃閃發光有如雪白的大城堡。
每一個人，是的，每一個人，
　　都在山頂上停了下來，望著聖殿，
　　望著那座美麗的聖殿。

The next day Mark and Sara and many other children
   went with Jesus and His friends to the Temple.
But when they got there,
   the sounds coming from the Temple
   didn't sound like a Temple at all.
There was no sound of singing and praying.
It wasn't quiet—like and hush-like,
   with people tiptoeing when they walked.
Instead—there was a terrible rackety noise!

隔天，馬可和撒拉，和其他的孩子們，
　　都跟著耶穌和祂的朋友們前往聖殿。
但是當他們到達那裏時，
　　有聲音從聖殿傳出來，
　　然而，這聲音一點都不像是聖殿該有的聲音。
沒有唱歌和禱告的聲音，
也沒有安靜——和莊嚴的氣氛，
　　更沒有讓人想踮著腳尖走路的感覺，
相反地——只有可怕的喧鬧聲！

140

Traders had brought to the Temple cattle
    and sheep and doves to sell for offerings.
They shouted, "Buy cattle for your offering."
"Buy sheep for your offering."
"Buy doves for your offering."
Moneychangers were there, clinking their money.
It didn't seem like a Temple at all–not at all.
It was like a noisy market place.

商人將牛、羊和鴿子帶到聖殿裏，
　賣給來獻祭的人們。
他們大聲吆喝：「來買牛獻祭啊！」
「來買羊獻祭啊！」
「來買鴿子獻祭啊！」
換銀錢的商人叮叮噹噹地數著他們的銀錢。
聖殿看起來簡直不像是聖殿——它一點都不像，
倒像是一個吵雜的市場。

Jesus stood in the doorway—
The cattle traders looked at Him.
The sheep traders looked at Him.
The dove traders looked at Him.
They all stopped their shouting and selling.
The moneychangers stopped clinking their money.
Everyone looked at Jesus and waited
    to see what He would do.
Jesus raised His arm.
He said, *"TAKE THESE THINGS HENCE!"*

耶穌站在門口——
賣牛的商人看著祂，
賣羊的商人看著祂，
賣鴿子的商人也看著祂，
他們都停止叫賣聲和買賣的動作。
換銀錢的商人也停止數算他們的銀錢。
每一個人都注視著耶穌，
　等著看祂會做出什麼事。
只見耶穌舉起手來，
大聲說：「把這些東西統統拿出去！」

Such a hurrying and a scurrying!
The traders hustled the cattle out.
They rushed the sheep out.
They grabbed the dove cages and ran.
The moneychangers didn't even stop to take their money.
All the grown-up people ran away from Jesus.

145

大家立刻亂成一團！
商人們急忙把他們的牛往外推。
他們趕緊將他們的羊趕出去。
他們隨手抓著他們的鴿子籠，拔腿就跑。
換銀錢的商人甚至來不及撿起地上的銀錢。
所有的商人都遠遠地從耶穌旁邊跑開了。

But the children didn't run away from Jesus.
Mark and Sara and all the children crowded close around Him.
Jesus told them stories.
He took the little ones on His knee.
A little boy, went to sleep on His lap.

但是小孩子並沒有離開耶穌。

馬可和撒拉，和其他的小孩們都靠過去，圍住耶穌。

耶穌講故事給他們聽。

祂讓小朋友緊挨在祂的膝旁，

一個小男孩坐在祂的腿上睡著了。

Then the sick people came to Jesus.
A boy with a hurt leg came hobbling on crutches.
Jesus put His hand on the hurt leg and made it well.
The boy threw away his crutches.
Now he could walk. He could run!
He could jump!

M. deV. Lee

沒多久，生病的人們來找耶穌。
有一位腿受傷的男孩拄著拐杖來。
耶穌把手按在他受傷的腿上，治好了它。
小男孩丟開他的柺杖，
現在他可以走路了。他可以跑了！
他還可以跳了！

151

M. de V. Lee

A father and mother brought their sick little girl to Jesus.
She was so sick they carried her in a hammock.
Jesus took her small thin hand in His. He said,
    "Be well, little girl, be well."
The little girl sat up and smiled. She was well.

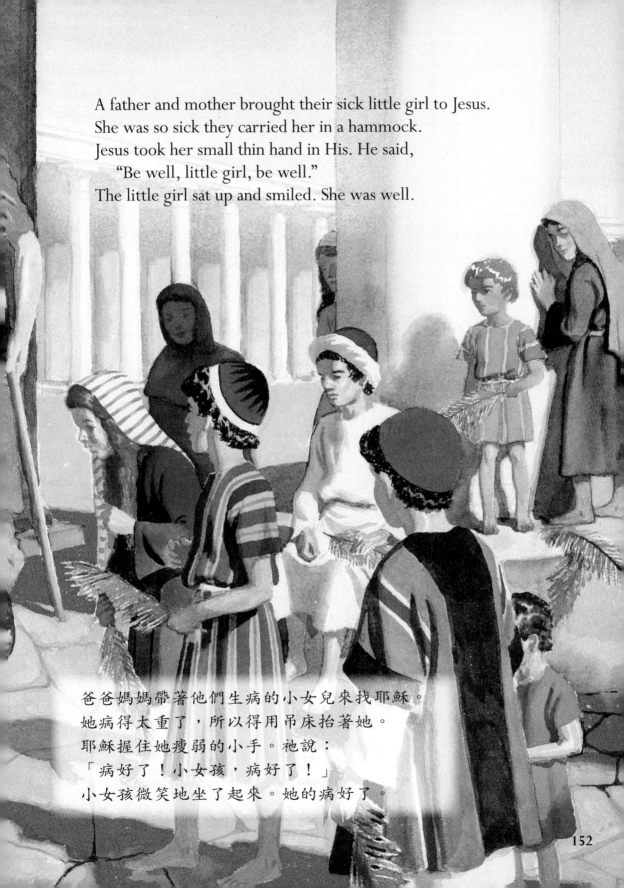

爸爸媽媽帶著他們生病的小女兒來找耶穌。
她病得太重了，所以得用吊床抬著她。
耶穌握住她瘦弱的小手。他說：
「病好了！小女孩，病好了！」
小女孩微笑地坐了起來。她的病好了。

A boy led a blind man to Jesus.
The blind man's eyes were tight shut.
He had never seen a tree or a house–not anything.
Jesus made his eyes see.
And the first thing the blind man ever saw
     was the lovely face of Jesus.

一個男孩領著一位瞎子來找耶穌。
那位瞎子的眼睛完全看不見東西。
他生平從沒看過一棵樹或一棟房子──什麼都沒看過。
耶穌使他重見光明。
那位瞎子第一眼所見到的，
　　就是耶穌慈愛的臉。

154

155

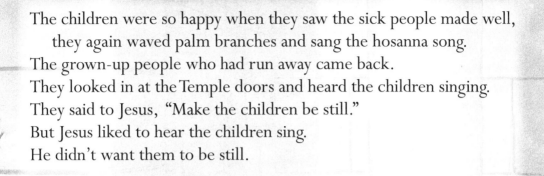

The children were so happy when they saw the sick people made well,
they again waved palm branches and sang the hosanna song.
The grown-up people who had run away came back.
They looked in at the Temple doors and heard the children singing.
They said to Jesus, "Make the children be still."
But Jesus liked to hear the children sing.
He didn't want them to be still.

孩子們很高興看見病人被治好了，
他們再次揮舞著棕櫚樹枝，唱著《和散那》的讚美歌。
那些逃跑的商人回來了。
他們在聖殿門口探頭探腦，聽見孩子們在唱歌。
他們對耶穌說：「叫那些孩子安靜下來！」
但是耶穌喜歡聽孩子們唱歌。
祂不想叫他們安靜下來。

157

It was time to close the Temple doors.
Tomorrow the children would come back to hear more stories.
Jesus wanted them to come. He had said,
    "Suffer the little children to come unto me,
    and forbid them not."

聖殿關門的時間到了。
明天這些小孩還想回來聽更多的故事。
耶穌要他們回來。祂曾說過：
    「讓這些小孩到我這裏來，
    不要禁止他們。」

158

M. de V. Lee

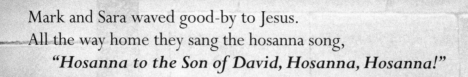

Mark and Sara waved good-by to Jesus.
All the way home they sang the hosanna song,
"Hosanna to the Son of David, Hosanna, Hosanna!"

馬可和撒拉向耶穌揮手道別。
在回家的路上，他們一直唱著《和散那》的讚美歌：
「和散那歸於大衛的子孫，和散那！和散那！」

最小的男孩大衛
David, the Youngest Boy

大衛是一位很會照顧羊群的好牧童，
他勇敢地用小石子趕走了兇猛的野熊。
但上帝對大衛另有計劃，祂要大衛做什麼事呢？

Eight brothers standing in a row!
The youngest boy at the end of the row is David.
David and his brothers lived on a farm near a small town.
David was a shepherd boy.
He took care of his father's sheep.

163

八個兄弟站成一排！
那位站在隊伍尾端，年紀最小的男孩就是大衛。
大衛和哥哥們住在小鎮附近的農莊裏。
大衛是個牧童，
他照顧爸爸的羊群。

To David's town came Samuel the prophet.
The prophet invited all the people to a special feast.
David's brothers were going to the feast.
David's father was going to the feast.
But the brothers said to David,
"You are too young to go.
You stay home
with the sheep."

165

先知撒母耳來到大衛住的小鎮。
先知邀請所有人出席一場特別的宴會。
大衛的哥哥們都準備赴宴。
大衛的爸爸也準備好要赴宴了。
但是，哥哥們對大衛說：
「你年紀太小了，不能赴宴。
　　你就好好待在家裏照顧羊群吧！」

David took his harp under his arm.
He tucked his sling in his belt.
He opened the gate to the sheeppen.
"Come, sheep! Come, lambs!" he called.
The sheep followed David down the path.
Black Lamb and Curly Lamb walked
　　one on each side of David.

大衛將豎琴夾在手臂下。
他把投石器塞進腰帶裏。
他打開羊欄的柵門。
「大羊，來吧！小羊，來吧！」他呼叫。
羊群跟著大衛走到小路上。
小黑羊和小捲毛羊各走在大衛的一旁。

168

David led the sheep to a green grassy place.
While the older sheep nibbled grass
　　Black Lamb and Curly Lamb,
　　played jumping games and bunting games
　　with the other lambs.
David played tunes on his harp
　　and kept close watch of the sheep.

大衛帶領羊群來到一片青草地上。
大羊細嚼青草時，
　　小黑羊與小捲毛羊就和其他的小羊
　　一起玩耍跳躍。
大衛一邊彈奏著豎琴，
　　一邊小心看顧著羊群。

Black Lamb began to wander away up over the hill.
David put down his harp and ran after him.
He brought Black Lamb back to the flock.
Then David saw a weed that would
    make the sheep sick if they ate it.
He pulled up the weed and threw it away.
A jackal sneaked around a rock toward the sheep.
David stamped his foot, and the jackal *ran*.

小黑羊開始在山丘上到處跑來跑去。

大衛放下他的豎琴，跑過去將牠追回來。

他把小黑羊帶回羊群中。

大衛看到一叢野草，

　如果羊吃到了這種野草，就會生病。

他把野草拔起來扔到一旁。

有一隻豺狼躲在岩石旁邊，牠偷偷走近羊群。

大衛用力跺著他的腳，豺狼便嚇跑了。

David took his sling from his belt.
It was a long, long sling that his father had made for him
　　from strong brown leather.
He put a smooth stone in the sling.
Now what should he hit? That red rock?
He would try.
Around and around and around he swung his sling.
Zing—g—g—g went the stone!
Ping! It hit the red rock.

大衛把腰間上的投石器拿出來。
那是一個很長、很長的投石器，是爸爸為他做的，
　　它是用很強韌的棕色皮革做成的。
他在投石器上放了一顆光滑的小石子。
他該投擊什麼東西呢？那塊紅色的岩石嗎？
他想要試試看！
轉了一圈又一圈，他用力甩動著投石器。
咻——咻——咻，石子飛出去了！
砰！它擊中了紅色的岩石。

David put another stone in his sling.
He would aim for that round black hole in the tree.
Around and around and around he swung the sling.
Zing–g–g–g went the stone straight into the round
　　black hole in the tree.

大衛又放了一顆小石子在投石器上。
他瞄準樹上的一個黑洞。
轉了一圈又一圈，他用力甩動著投石器。
咻——咻——咻，石頭飛出去了，
　　石子準確地打進了樹上那個圓圓的黑洞裏。

175

Then David heard a noise.
It wasn't a **hopping, thumping** noise
    like a rabbit running
    through the grass.
No…it wasn't a rabbit.

It wasn't a **picking**,
    pecking noise
    like a bird pecking on a tree.
No…it wasn't a bird.

It was a **sn–uffing, gr–r–ruffing** noise
    like a big animal prowling around.
It was—

177

過一會兒，大衛聽到一個聲音。
這聲音不像是兔子跳過草叢的砰砰聲。
不…它不是兔子。

它也不像是小鳥在啄樹的咚咚聲。
不…它不是小鳥。

碰—碰—的聲音好像是一隻大動物
　　在附近覓食的聲音。
那是——

A **BEAR**! A fierce brown bear!
And he was sneaking closer, and closer, and closer,
    to where the lambs were playing.
The bear crept up behind a bush
    ready to snatch Curly Lamb
    as she ran by.

一隻熊！一隻兇猛的棕熊！
牠偷偷靠近小羊玩耍的地方，
　越來越近，越走越近。
這隻熊慢慢潛行到樹叢後方，
　準備趁小捲毛羊走過去的時候，
　一把抓住她。

Quickly David put a stone in his sling.
He ran straight toward the bear.
Around and around and around he swung the sling.
Zing—g—g—g went the stone!
It hit the fierce brown bear. The bear fell dead.

大衛趕緊放了一顆石子在投石器上，
他朝著那隻熊跑過去。
轉了一圈又一圈，他用力甩動著投石器。
咻──咻──咻，石子飛了出去！
石子擊中兇猛的棕熊。熊立刻倒地死了。

David picked up frightened little Curly Lamb and
    carried her in his arms.
Black Lamb kept close by his side.
"Come sheep! Come lambs!" called David,
    and he led them to a place where they would be safe.
while the older sheep nibbled the new green grass,
    Black Lamb and Curly Lamb again played jumping games
    with the other lambs, and David played tunes on his harp.

大衛抱起被嚇壞的小捲毛羊，
    小黑羊緊挨在他身旁。
「大羊，來吧！小羊，來吧！」大衛呼叫。
    他將牠們帶到安全的地方。
大羊嚼著新鮮的嫩草時，
    小黑羊，小捲毛羊和別的小羊又開始玩耍起來了，
    大衛也開始彈奏起他的豎琴。

Now while David was watching the sheep,
    Samuel the prophet made ready the feast.
David's father was at the feast.
David's brothers were at the feast.
Before they sat down to eat,
    the prophet said to David's father,
"Have your boys walk before me, one by one.
Today God will choose one of them
    for something very special."

就在大衛看顧羊群的時候，
　先知撒母耳準備好宴席了。
大衛的爸爸在席上，
大衛的哥哥們也在席上，
就在他們用餐之前，
　先知對大衛的爸爸說：
「叫你的兒子一個一個走過我的面前。
今天上帝將從他們當中揀選一人，
　做非常特別的工作。」

186

David's oldest brother walked before the prophet.
"No, it is not this boy," said the prophet.
The next oldest brother walked before the prophet.
"No, it is not this boy," said the prophet.
And then the next oldest brother walked before the prophet.
The prophet shook his head. "No, it is not this boy."

大衛的大哥從先知面前走過。

「不，不是這個男孩。」先知說。

二哥從先知面前走過。

「不，不是這個男孩。」先知說。

三哥從先知面前走過。

先知搖搖頭說：「不，也不是這個男孩。」

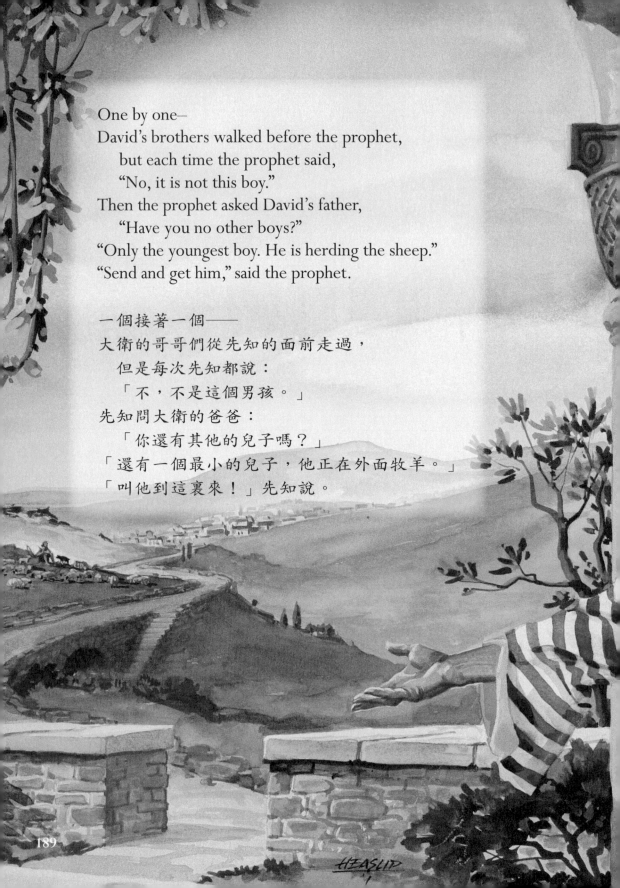

One by one—
David's brothers walked before the prophet,
   but each time the prophet said,
   "No, it is not this boy."
Then the prophet asked David's father,
   "Have you no other boys?"
"Only the youngest boy. He is herding the sheep."
"Send and get him," said the prophet.

一個接著一個──
大衛的哥哥們從先知的面前走過，
   但是每次先知都說：
   「不，不是這個男孩。」
先知問大衛的爸爸：
   「你還有其他的兒子嗎？」
「還有一個最小的兒子，他正在外面牧羊。」
「叫他到這裏來！」先知說。

189

David came running,
　　his harp under his arm,
　　his sling in his belt.
His cheeks were red.
The wind blew his hair.

大衛一路跑過來，
　　他的手臂下夾著豎琴，
　　他的投石器繫在腰帶。
他的雙頰紅潤。
微風吹拂著他的頭髮。

192

"Walk before the prophet, David," said his father.
David walked before the prophet. "This is the one,"
    said the prophet. "This is the boy God chooses."
The prophet poured sweet-smelling oil
    on David's head to show that he was the chosen one.

「大衛，從先知面前走過去。」他的爸爸說。
大衛就從先知面前走過。「就是他！」先知說，
    「這個男孩就是上帝揀選的人。」
先知將芬芳的油倒在大衛的頭上，
    證明他就是被上帝揀選的人。

"Now we shall sit down to the feast," said the prophet.
A place was made for David,
    and he sat with his father and brothers.
Why had David been chosen? What would he do?
No one knew. It was a secret. David's father didn't know.
David's brothers didn't know. David didn't know.
Only the prophet and God knew that someday—

「現在我們可以坐下來用餐了。」先知說。
有一個座位是留給大衛坐的，
　　他坐在爸爸和哥哥們的旁邊。
為什麼上帝會揀選大衛？他將來要做什麼事呢？
沒有人知道，它是一個祕密。大衛的爸爸不知道。
大衛的哥哥們不知道，連大衛自己也不知道。
只有先知和上帝知道，將來有一天──

David would be **KING**.
And David would be as good a king
as he was a shepherd boy.

大衛將來會成為一名國王。
並且大衛會成為一位好國王，
就像他是個好牧童一樣。

去河裏沐浴
Go Wash in the River

威武的乃縵將軍得了痲瘋病，
國內沒有任何醫生可以治好他，
小婢女說只有先知以利沙可以醫治他的病，
但他願意聽從先知的話嗎？

199

Little Maid was far, far from home.
She worked for Captain and Lady Naaman.
She washed dishes. She ran errands.
Little Maid did everything
Captain and Lady Naaman asked her to do,
   except one thing.
One thing Little Maid did not do.

小婢女離家很遠很遠。
她為乃縵將軍和他的夫人工作。
她洗盤子，還做許多雜務。
無論乃縵將軍和夫人吩咐她去做任何事，
小婢女都會去做，
　　除了一件事。
那一件事小婢女不會去做。

Captain and Lady Naaman prayed to an idol,
   an ugly stone idol.
The idol couldn't see. It couldn't hear.
When Captain and Lady Naaman asked Little Maid
   to pray with them to the idol,
Little Maid said, "Oh, no, I cannot pray to an idol.
   I pray to the God in heaven.
   He sees me. He hears me."

乃縵將軍和夫人平時都會拜一座雕像，
　　那是一座醜陋的石雕像。
那座雕像看不見，也聽不見。
當乃縵將軍和夫人要求小婢女
　　和他們一起拜那座雕像時，
小婢女會說：「不！不，我不拜雕像。
　　我只向天上的上帝禱告。
　　祂看得見我，也聽得見我的聲音。」

One morning when Little Maid
	took Lady Naaman her breakfast,
	Lady Naaman was crying.
"Why do you cry?" asked Little Maid.
"Captain Naaman is sick. He has leprosy spots.
	The doctors cannot make him well."

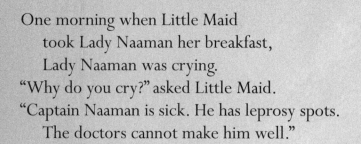

有一天早晨，
	小婢女為乃縵夫人端來早餐，
	乃縵夫人正在哭。
「你為什麼哭呢？」小婢女問。
「乃縵將軍病了，他得了痲瘋病。
	所有的醫生都沒辦法治好他。」

"I know someone," said Little Maid, "who can make
Captain Naaman well. If he will go
to the prophet at my home, far, far away,
the prophet will know what to do
to make him well."
Lady Naaman told Captain Naaman
what Little Maid said.

「我知道有一個人，」小婢女說，
　「他能夠治好將軍的病。
　如果將軍能到我遠方的家鄉，
　找到那位先知，
　這位先知就能把他治好。」
乃緩夫人將小婢女所說的話，
　告訴乃緩將軍。

208

"I will go see the prophet," said Captain Naaman.
"I will take him presents."
Captain Naaman rode in his best chariot.
He drove his fastest horses.
Men on horseback rode along behind the chariot.
At the turn of the road
    Captain Naaman waved good-by to Lady Naaman.
He waved good-by to Little Maid.

「我要去見那位先知，」乃縵將軍說，
「我會送許多禮物給他。」
乃縵將軍跳上他最好的馬車，
駕著他最快的馬。
士兵們也騎著馬跟在他的馬車後面。
在路口轉彎的地方，
    乃縵將軍向夫人揮手道別，
他也揮手向小婢女道別。

The prophet saw Captain Naaman
    and his men coming down the road.
He had heard about Captain Naaman's sickness.
He sent a man to meet him and tell him what to do.
"Tell Captain Naaman," said the prophet,
    "to go wash in the river Jordan seven times,
    and he will be well."

先知看到乃縵將軍，
　和他的士兵迎面而來。
他已經聽說乃縵將軍的病情了，
他便派了一名僕人去見乃縵將軍，告訴他該怎麼做。
「告訴乃縵將軍，」先知對僕人說，
　「他只要去約旦河沐浴七次，
　就會好起來。」

212

Captain Naaman said to his men,
  "Does the prophet think I am dirty?
  Does he think I need a bath?
  I will **not** wash in that muddy river."
Captain Naaman was angry, very angry,
  because the prophet told him
  to go wash in the river.
"I will go home," said Caaptain Naaman.

乃縵將軍對他手下的人說：
　　「難道先知認為我很髒嗎？
　　難道他認為我需要洗澡嗎？
　　我絕不會去那條混濁的河裏沐浴。」
乃縵將軍很生氣，非常生氣，
　　因為先知要他去那條河裏沐浴。
「我要回家！」乃縵將軍說。

Captain Naaman started home.
The men on horseback rode up close beside him.
They said to him, "If the prophet had asked
    you to do some big thing,
    wouldn't you have done it?
    Why don't you do this little thing?
    Why don't you do wash in the river?"
Captain Naaman drove slower.
At last he turned off the road,
    and drove down toward the river.

乃縵將軍說完，立刻啟程回家。

騎在馬背上的士兵們，趕到他身邊。

他們對他說：「如果先知要求你做一些大事，

　　你難道不會去做嗎？

　　為什麼這一點點小事你卻不想去做呢？

　　為何你不去河裏沐浴呢？」

乃縵將軍放慢了速度。

最後，他終於調轉方向，

　　朝著河邊騎去。

The river was muddy,
   but Captain Naaaman waded out into it.
He dipped down under the water.
Then he looked at his hands and his arms.
The leprosy spots were still there.

河水很混濁，
　但是乃縵將軍仍然涉水走進河裏。
他將身子浸泡在水中。
他看看自己的手和手臂，
那些痲瘋病的斑塊仍然存在。

218

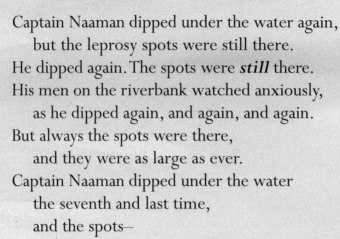

Captain Naaman dipped under the water again,
    but the leprosy spots were still there.
He dipped again. The spots were *still* there.
His men on the riverbank watched anxiously,
    as he dipped again, and again, and again.
But always the spots were there,
    and they were as large as ever.
Captain Naaman dipped under the water
    the seventh and last time,
    and the spots—

乃縵將軍再一次浸泡在水裏，
　　但是痲瘋病的斑塊仍在。
他又浸泡了一次。斑塊仍然存在。
他的士兵們在岸邊焦急地看著，
　　他一次又一次，一次又一次。
但是那些斑塊還是在原處，
　　並且斑塊跟先前的一樣大。
乃縵將軍在第七次，
　　也是最後一次，浸泡在水中，
　　那些斑塊——

The spots were **GONE!**
Captain Naaman looked at his hands.
He looked at his legs.
He looked all over his body,
    but not a single spot could he find.
The spots were all gone. He was **WELL!**
His men clapped their hands and cheered.

那些斑塊統統不見了！
乃縵將軍看看自己的雙手，
又看看自己的雙腿。
他仔細檢查全身上下，
　連一塊斑都沒找到。
斑塊全消失了。他的病好了！
他的士兵們高興地鼓掌歡呼。

Captain Naaman ran splashing out of the river.
He jumped into his chariot.
He galloped his horses back to the prophet's house
    to tell him thank you.
All of his men galloped along with him.

乃縵將軍從河裏衝上來，濺起好多水花。
他急忙跳上馬車，
駕著他的馬車，朝著先知的家飛奔而去，
　他要跟先知說聲謝謝。
士兵們也都跟著他一路疾奔。

Captain Naaman bowed low before the prophet,
  and thanked him.
He offered him the presents he had brought.
But the prophet said, "I cannot take the presents.
  I did not make you well.
  It was the God in heaven who made you well."

乃縵將軍在先知的面前深深地鞠了一個躬，
　向他道謝。
他把帶來的許多禮物送給先知。
但是先知說：「我不能收你的禮物。
　不是我治好你的病，
　是天上的上帝治好你的病。」

Captain Naaman and his men hurried home.
Lady Naaman and Little Maid
    were watching the road.
Captain Naaman waved to them. He drove faster.
When he came near he shouted,
    "I am well! I am well!"

乃縵將軍和他的士兵們連忙趕路回家。
乃縵夫人和小婢女兩人，
　　一直眺望著街道。
乃縵將軍向她們揮手。他騎得更快了。
當他快到家時，他立刻大叫：
　　「我的病好了！我的病好了！」

And now when Captain and Lady Naaman prayed,
  they didn't pray to the idol
  that couldn't see and couldn't hear.
They prayed to the God in heaven,
  and Little Maid prayed with them.
"Thank You, God in heaven,"
  prayed Captain Naaman,
  "Thank You for making me well."

現在，當乃縵將軍和夫人禱告的時候，
　他們不再對著那個看不見、
　也聽不見的雕像禱告了。
他們向著天上的上帝禱告，
　小婢女也和他們一起禱告。
「謝謝你，在天上的上帝，」
　乃縵將軍真誠地祈禱，
　「謝謝你治好了我的病。」

以利亞和
乾旱的日子

Elijah, and the Time
of No-Rain

上帝派先知以利亞去警告邪惡的亞哈王，說
天不下雨，也不降露，
直到祂的百姓遠離偶像。
亞哈王聽了非常生氣，就派兵到處捉拿以利亞⋯⋯

King Ahab was a **wicked** king.
He set up idols of Baal, and altars of Baal,
    along the paths in the woods.
"Pray to Baal," he said to the people. "Baal sends
    the rain to make your fields and gardens grow."
King Ahab built a beautiful temple.
He placed the ugly idol of Baal in the temple.
"Pray to Baal," he said. "Baal sends the rain."

亞哈王是一個邪惡的國王。

他造了許多巴力的雕像，

　還沿著森林小路蓋了許多巴力的祭壇

「向巴力神祈禱，」他對百姓說，

　「巴力神會賜下雨水，讓你們的莊稼和蔬菜能夠生長。」

亞哈王又建造了一座輝煌的廟宇。

他將醜陋的巴力雕像安放在廟裏。

「向巴力神祈禱，」他說，

　「巴力神會賜下雨水給你們。」

Prophet Elijah looked down from the mountains
where he lived in a little house built of stones.
He saw the temple of Baal. It made him weep.
God came near, and talked with Prophet Elijah.
"I will teach the king and the people
that it is I, the Lord, who sends the rain,
not the idol Baal. Go tell King Ahab," He said,
"that there will be neither dew nor rain until
The people of Israel turn away from idols."

先知以利亞住在山上，
　他從山上的小石屋往下看。
他看到了巴力的廟宇，這讓他痛心流淚。
上帝來找先知以利亞，向他說話。
　「我要教導亞哈王和百姓，
　賜下雨水的是我，耶和華，
　不是那個偶像巴力。
　去告訴亞哈王我所說的，」祂說，
　「天將不下雨，也不降露，
　直到以色列人遠離那些偶像。」

Down the mountainside hurried Prophet Elijah.
Across the valley to the king's palace,
    past the king's soldiers......Elijah
        did not stop until he stood before King Ahab.
"As the Lord God liveth," he told the king,
    "there shall be neither dew nor rain until
        the people of Israel turn away from idols."
Then Prophet Elijah quickly left the king's palace.
God whispered to him—
    "Hide yourself beside the Brook Cherith."

先知以利亞急忙下山。

他橫越山谷，來到皇宮，

　經過國王的衛兵……

　以利亞沒有停下腳步，他一直走到亞哈王的面前。

「我指著永生的上帝起誓，」他對亞哈王說，

　「天不下雨，也不降露，

　直到以色列的百姓遠離偶像。」

說完，先知以利亞立刻離開皇宮。

上帝對他輕聲低語——

　「你趕快到基立溪附近躲起來。」

238

"Catch Elijah! Stop him! " shouted the king.
"Don't let him get away!"
But Elijah was already gone.
The soldiers ran in all directions to find him.
They went to his mountain home,
    but Elijah was not there.
They hunted for him in the fields,
    but Elijah was not there.
Even King Ahab Joined in the search,
    but no one could find Prophet Elijah.

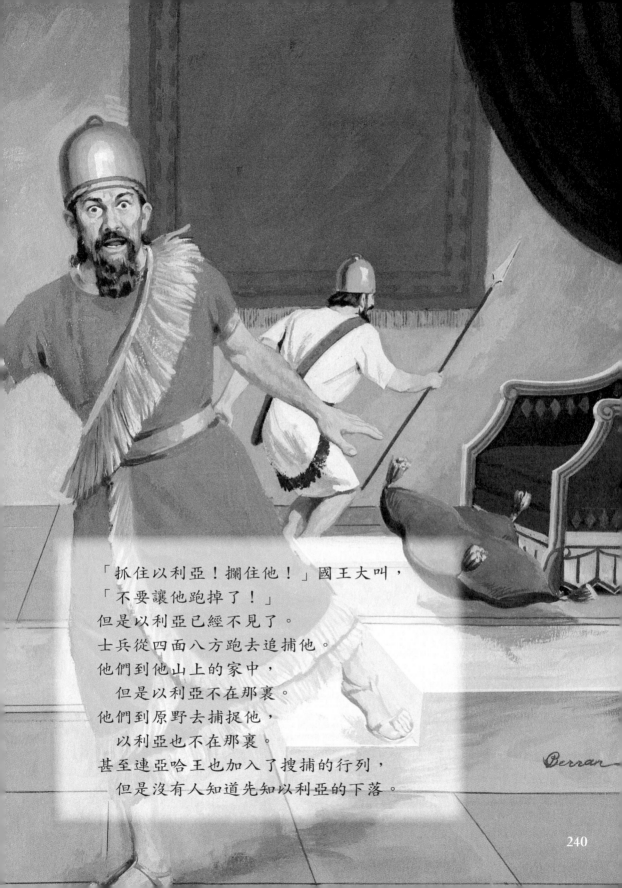

「抓住以利亞！攔住他！」國王大叫，
「不要讓他跑掉了！」
但是以利亞已經不見了。
士兵從四面八方跑去追捕他。
他們到他山上的家中，
　　但是以利亞不在那裏。
他們到原野去捕捉他，
　　以利亞也不在那裏。
甚至連亞哈王也加入了搜捕的行列，
　　但是沒有人知道先知以利亞的下落。

240

Elijah hid beside the Brook Cherith.
He drank the clear, cool water of the Brook Cherith.
Every morning, after the sun came up,
   and every evening, before the sun went down,
      God sent ravens to bring him food.
Many, many days Elijah lived beside Brook Cherith.
The wild creatures became his friends.

以利亞就躲在基立溪旁邊。
他喝基立溪裏乾淨又清涼的溪水。
每天早晨，在日出之後，
   和每天傍晚，在日落之前，
      上帝都差派烏鴉為他送來食物。
以利亞在基立溪旁邊住了好多、好多天。
動物們都成為他的朋友了。

Because there was no rain,
    the grass turned brown,
    the leaves fell from the trees,
    and there was no grain to harvest.
Finally the Brook Cherith dried up,
    and there was no water for Elijah to drink.
But God did not forget him–God never forgets.
"Go to the city of Zerephath," He told Elijah.
"I have commanded a widow who lives there
    to give you food and water."

因為天不下雨，
　　地上的綠草枯黃了，
　　樹上的樹葉掉光了，
　　沒有穀物可以收成。
最後連基立溪也乾涸了，
　　沒有溪水可以給以利亞喝。
但是上帝並沒有忘記他──上帝從不會忘記。
「到撒勒法城去，」祂告訴以利亞。
「我已經吩咐住在那裏的一名寡婦，
　　為你準備了食物和水。」

The widow of Zerephath was searching for wood
near the city gate when Prophet Elijah came by.
Elijah asked her for a drink and some bread.
Said the widow, "I have only a handful of meal
and a little oil. I am gathering two sticks
to bake the last loaf of bread for me
and my boy; after that we must die."

"Fear not," said Elijah,
"make me a little cake,
for God has said that
the meal shall not lack,
nor the oil fail
until the day
He sends rain."

先知以利亞來到撒勒法城的時候，
　　寡婦正在城門旁邊撿木柴。
以利亞向她討一些水和餅吃。
寡婦說：「我只剩一把麵粉和一點油。
　　我打算撿幾根木柴，
　　為自己和兒子烤好這最後的一個餅，
　　之後我們就準備等死了。」
「不要擔心，」以利亞說，
　　「先做一塊小餅給我吃，
　　因為上帝跟我說，
　　麵粉不會缺少，
　　油也不會缺少，
　　直到祂賜下雨水的那一天為止。」

The widow baked a little cake for Prophet Elijah,
    and drew him a drink from the well;
    she gave him a room in the loft of her home.
And it happened as God had said.
Every morning there was a handful
    of meal in her barrel,
    and a little oil in her cruse—
    enough for the day's loaf of bread—
    and God sent water in the well.
So, during the time of no-rain,
    the widow, the boy,
    and Elijah had bread to eat
    and water to drink.

247

寡婦烤了一塊小餅給以利亞吃，
　並且從井裏提了一些水給他喝；
　她又在屋子的閣樓整理了一個房間給他住。
事情就像上帝所說的。
每天早晨，都有一把麵粉出現
　在寡婦的桶子裏，
　還有一些油在她的罐子裏──
　足夠做這一天他們所需要吃的餅──
　並且，上帝也在井裏預備了一些水。
所以，在乾旱的日子裏，
　寡婦和她的兒子，
　還有以利亞，都有餅可以吃，
　也有水可以喝。

Three years of no-rain went by.
Then one day God said to Prophet Elijah,
    "Go, show yourself unto King Ahab,
    and I will send rain upon the earth."
Back to the land of Israel went Prophet Elijah.
He met King Ahab on a path. The king frowned at him.
"Is it you, you troubler of Israel?"
"I have not troubled Israel," said Elijah. "You have,
    because you turned away from God. Gather
    all the people of Israel to me on Mount Carmel,"
    commanded Elijah, "and all the prophets of Baal."

三年乾旱的日子過去了。
有一天，上帝告訴先知以利亞：
    「去！告訴亞哈王，
    我將為大地降下雨水。」
於是，先知以利亞回到以色列。
他在路上遇見了亞哈王。國王皺皺眉頭看著他說：
「是你，是你把這場災難帶給以色列的嗎？」
「為以色列帶來災難的不是我，是你！」以利亞說，
    「因為你遠離了上帝。
    現在召集所有以色列的百姓，
    到迦密山去見我，」以利亞下令，
    「所有巴力的先知也要去。」

King Ahab did as Prophet Elijah said—
    all the people of Israel, and all the prophets of Baal,
    gathered together on Mount Carmel.
This day Elijah would prove who was the **true** God.
"Let us build two altars," said Elijah,
    "one to the Lord, and one to Baal. Let us place
    wood on the altars, and an offering upon the wood.
    The God who answers by fire—HE IS GOD."
All the people answered, "It is well spoken."

亞哈王照著先知以利亞的話去做──

　　所有以色列的百姓和巴力的先知們，

　　都聚集在迦密山上。

這一天以利亞將會證明誰才是**真正的上帝**。

「我們來搭建兩座祭壇，」以利亞說，

　　「一座給上帝，一座給巴力。

　　我們把木柴放到祭壇上，再把祭物放在木柴上。」

　　能從天上降下火來回應祈求的神──**就是真正的上帝**。

所有人都回答：「說得好！」

The prophets of Baal built their altar.
They placed wood on the altar, and an offering upon the wood.
They prayed to Baal from morning until noon,
 "O Baal, hear us. Hear us, O Baal. "There was no answer.
They cried louder and louder; they leaped and
 they jumped around the altar; they cut themselves.
Still there was no answer.

巴力的先知造了他們的祭壇。

他們將木柴放到祭壇上，再將祭物放到木柴上。

從早上到中午，他們不斷地向巴力祈求：

　　「哦！巴力神啊！請聽我們的祈求。哦！巴力神啊！」但是沒有任何回應。

他們的呼求聲越來越大；

　　他們圍著祭壇又叫又跳，又用刀子割自己的身體。

但是仍然沒有任何回應。

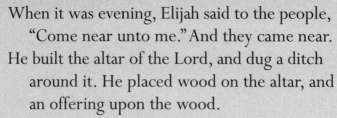

When it was evening, Elijah said to the people,
   "Come near unto me." And they came near.
He built the altar of the Lord, and dug a ditch
   around it. He placed wood on the altar, and
   an offering upon the wood.
Then water was poured over the altar;
   it ran down and filled the ditch.
The people watched and waited.
Looking toward heaven, Elijah prayed,
            "O Lord God, let it be known this day
            that thou art God......"

到了傍晚，以利亞向那些百姓說：

「到我這裏來。」於是他們靠了過去。

他為上帝造了一個祭壇，在它的周圍挖了一道溝。

他在祭壇上放上木柴，然後將祭物放在木柴上。

再叫人將水倒在祭壇上；

水從祭壇上流下來，注滿了溝。

百姓在旁邊注視著，等待著。

以利亞仰望天上，禱告說：

「哦！主，我的上帝啊，這一天就讓大家知道

你才是真正的上帝……。」

Almost before Elijah could say *Amen*,
    fire flashed down from heaven like lightning.
It burned up the offering. It burned up the wood.
It even burned up the stones of the altar,
    and the water in the ditch.
All the people shouted—"THE LORD, HE IS GOD!
    THE LORD, HE IS DOD!"
God heard them, and was pleased. That night
    He sent a great rain to water the earth.

幾乎就在以利亞要說阿們的時候，
　　一陣火從天上降下來，像一道閃電一樣。
這陣火燒盡了祭品和木柴，
它甚至燒掉祭壇的石頭，
　　也燒乾了溝裏的水。
所有的百姓都叫喊：「耶和華，祂是上帝！
　　耶和華，祂是上帝！」
上帝聽見他們的歡呼聲，就非常開心。
　　就在當天晚上，祂降下了一場大雨，滋潤大地。

258

耶穌和孩子們
Jesus and the Children

1 耶穌喜歡說故事給小朋友聽，你覺得耶穌是怎樣的一個人？

2 有人在聖殿做買賣，也弄髒了神聖的聖殿，耶穌當時的心情如何？

3 耶穌喜歡聽馬可和撒拉快樂的歌聲，你也喜歡唱詩歌給耶穌聽嗎？

最小的男孩大衛
David, the Youngest Boy

1 大衛是個什麼個性的小孩？你覺得他順服又勇敢嗎？

2 為什麼哥哥們放心把看顧羊群這麼重要的事，交給最小的弟弟大衛去做呢？

3 為何上帝要選擇大衛長大後當國王？他有沒有當國王的能力呢？

4 你知道上帝怎麼安排你未來的工作嗎？你也禱告問上帝吧！

去河裏沐浴
Go Wash in the River

1 乃縵貴為一名將軍，怎麼會聽一個小婢女的建議呢？ 是不是這個小婢女平常表現不一樣呢？

2 為什麼先知要乃縵將軍到約旦河洗七次澡，而不是一次或兩次呢？

3 為什麼先知不接受乃縵將軍答謝的禮物呢？

4 如果士兵們不把生氣的乃縵將軍追回來，乃縵將軍的痳瘋病還能得到醫治嗎？

5 如果你接受了耶穌的愛，你也會把耶穌介紹給朋友或家人嗎？

以利亞和乾旱的日子
Elilah, and the Time of No-Rain

1 天若沒下雨，地上變乾旱，人類生存的環境會有什麼危機？

2 為什麼巴力的先知求雨的時候，巴力卻不能讓天下雨？

3 以利亞求雨的時候，是誰讓天降雨了呢？

4 拜假神，或拜真神上帝，對你的生活有什麼不同？

261

M. deV. Lee

大麥餅與魚
Barley Loaves and Fishes

少年人開開心心地帶著午餐籃去聽耶穌講故事，
中午到了，但草地上的人們沒有食物可吃，
耶穌請這名少年跟大家分享他的五餅二魚，
突然間，他的食物變多了……

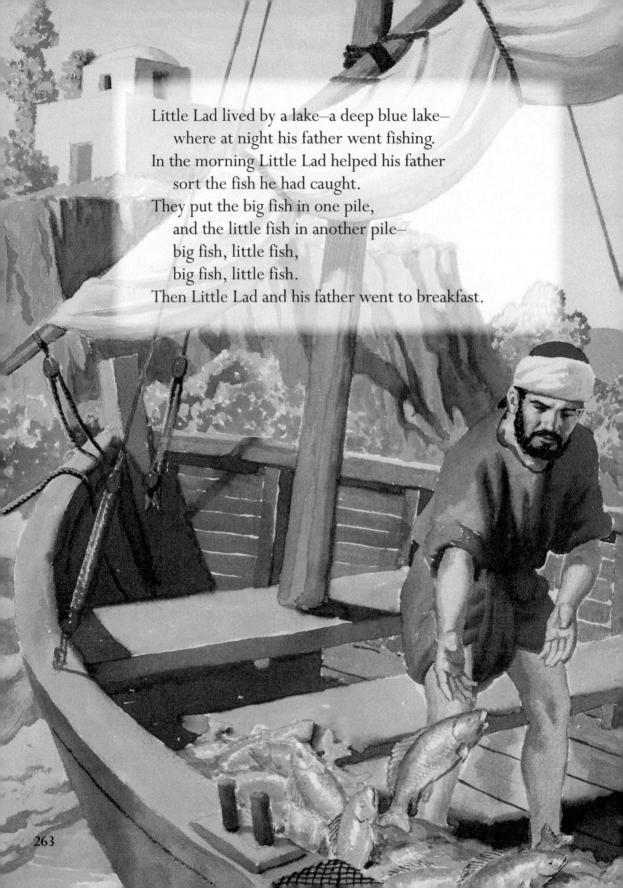

Little Lad lived by a lake—a deep blue lake—
  where at night his father went fishing.
In the morning Little Lad helped his father
  sort the fish he had caught.
They put the big fish in one pile,
  and the little fish in another pile—
  big fish, little fish,
  big fish, little fish.
Then Little Lad and his father went to breakfast.

有一個少年人住在湖邊——那是一座湖水深藍的湖——
　　晚上到了，他的爸爸就到湖裏打魚。
到了早上，少年人會幫爸爸的忙，
　　把捕到的魚分成好幾堆。
他們將大魚堆成一堆，
　　將小魚堆成一堆——
　　大魚、小魚，
　　大魚、小魚。
分完魚堆後，少年人就和爸爸去吃早餐。

For breakfast Little Lad barley loaves.
Little Lad liked barley loaves.
They were round and crusty and good.
Barley loaves would make him grow strong,
    make him grow tall.
Then he, too, could go fishing on the lake.

少年吃大麥餅當早餐。
他喜歡吃大麥餅。
它們圓圓脆脆的，又好吃。
大麥餅可以讓他長得更壯，
　還會讓他長得更高。
這樣，他也能去湖裏捕魚了。

One morning Little Lad saw many, many people
   going by his home along the lake shore.
They were going to find Jesus.
"May I go too?" he asked his mother.
"Why yes, you may go. I will make you a lunch.
   You will be hungry after that long walk."

有一天早晨，少年看見好多、好多的人，
　經過他家門口，沿著湖邊走過去。
原來他們是要去找耶穌。
「我也可以去嗎？」他問媽媽。
「當然可以！你可以去！我會為你準備午餐。
　走了那麼長的路之後，你一定會肚子餓的。」媽媽說。

Into a basket Little Lad's mother
    put five barley loaves and two small fishes.
She gave the basket to Little Lad
    to take with him on his long walk beside the lake.

少年的媽媽在籃子裏面
    放了五塊餅和兩條小魚。
她將籃子交給少年，
    讓他帶著籃子沿著湖岸走那條長路。

Little Lad waved good-by to his mother.
Barefooted, he walked through the tickly grass,
    and the prickly weeds, and over the sun-warmed stones.
Little Lad was happy—
    happy to be walking along the lake shore
    on such a sunny morning—
    but most of all he was happy because he was going to see Jesus.

少年向媽媽揮手說再見。
他赤腳走過令人發癢的草地，
    和多刺的雜草，還有被太陽曬得很暖和的石頭。
少年很開心——
    他很開心能夠在這麼晴朗的早晨
    沿著湖岸走——
    但最叫他開心的，是他要去見耶穌了。

272

M. deV. Lee

Little Lad found Jesus on a grassy hillside
    talking to many, many people.
Jesus told such interesting stories.
He told about animals, and birds,
    and what it is like up in heaven.
Little Lad listened, and listened.
Sometimes he thought of eating his lunch,
    but always he waited
    for just one more story.

他看見耶穌坐在山坡的草地上，
　對著好多、好多的人講話。
耶穌說了許多非常有趣的故事。
祂談到動物、鳥類，
　還有天國像什麼。
少年聽著，聽著入神了。
儘管有時候他想要吃他的午餐，
　但他還是繼續等待，
　因為他想要再多聽一個故事。

274

"Little Lad, do you have any lunch?"
    asked a man named Andrew.
"Oh, yes sir, I have five barley loaves and two small fishes."
"Would you like to share your lunch with Jesus?" asked Andrew.
"Oh, yes sir, I would like to share my lunch with Jesus."

「少年人，你有帶午餐來嗎？」
    一位名叫安得烈的男子問他。
「噢，是的，先生，我有五塊大麥餅和兩條小魚。」
「你願意與耶穌分享你的午餐嗎？」安得烈問。
「噢，是的，先生，我很願意與耶穌分享我的午餐。」

Little Lad gave his lunch basket to Andrew.
He watched Andrew take it to Jesus.
He saw the pleased look on Jesus' face.
And then he heard Jesus say to the people,
"Sit down on the grass, all of you.
We shall now have lunch."

277

少年人將他的午餐籃子交給安得烈。

他看著安得烈將籃子拿給耶穌。

他看見耶穌臉上喜悅的表情。

他聽到耶穌向群眾說：

「你們所有的人，先在草地上坐下來。

我們現在要吃午餐了。」

Little Lad's eyes opened wide......
He thought, "There is not enough lunch
    for all these people in my little lunch basket."
He was about to go and tell Jesus that there were only five
    barley loaves and two small fishes in the basket,
    but Jesus was asking the blessing. Little Lad bowed his head.

少年瞪大了眼睛……
他心想：「我那小小的午餐籃裏的食物，
    根本不夠給這麼多人吃！」
他正想跑去告訴耶穌，
    籃子裏只有五塊大麥餅和兩條小魚，
    但是耶穌已經在作飯前禱告了，少年只好低下頭跟著禱告。

M.deV.Lee

Little Lad saw Jesus reach into the basket and bring out
    barley loaves and fishes for His helpers to pass to the people.
Little Lad moved closer to see better.
Andrew smiled and gave him a loaf and a fish.
Then Jesus reached into the basket again
    and brought out more loaves and fishes.

Again, and again, and again,
Jesus put His hand into the basket
and always there were loaves
and fishes.

少年看見耶穌伸手到籃子裏，
　拿出了大麥餅和魚，遞給祂的助手，讓他們分給群眾。
少年走近一點，想看得更清楚。
安得烈微笑地遞給他一塊餅和一條魚。
接著，耶穌又伸手到籃子裏，
　拿出更多的餅和魚。
一次又一次，一次又一次的，
耶穌伸手到籃子裏，
　裏面總是有餅
　和魚出現。

283

M.deV.Lee

"How can it be?" thought Little Lad.
"In my basket there were only five loaves and two small fishes,
    but Jesus keeps taking out more, and more, and more."
And then he knew!
It was Jesus' **blessing** that made more—
    more barley loaves, more fishes.

「怎麼會這樣呢？」少年思索著。
「我的籃子裏明明只有五塊餅和兩條小魚啊！
    但是耶穌卻拿出更多、更多，還有更多的食物。」
這下子他明白了！
原來是耶穌的**祝福**，才會出現更多的食物──
    更多的大麥餅和更多的魚。

When everyone had eaten, Jesus said,
  "Gather up the leftover food."
His helpers went here and there with baskets
  picking up all the small pieces.
Little Lad counted the baskets of leftovers.
  "1, 2, 3, 4, 5, 6,......12 *baskets!*"
What a surprise–and all from his little lunch basket.

大家吃飽了之後，耶穌說：

「把剩餘的食物都收集起來。」

祂的助手們拿著籃子，

到處去收集剩餘的食物。

少年數了數裝著剩餘食物的籃子。

「1、2、3、4、5、6……12個籃子！」

太令人驚訝了——這些食物都來自他那小小的午餐籃子。

Little Lad hurried home
to tell his father and his mother
how Jesus had fed a big crowd of people
from his basket of lunch.
And how when the people had eaten,
there was more left over than he had to begin with.

少年趕緊跑回家去，
告訴他的爸爸和媽媽，
耶穌如何用他的一籃午餐，
餵飽了一大群人。
還有，大家吃飽之後，
剩餘的食物比剛開始他所給的五餅二魚，還要多出很多。

M.deV.Lee

少年國王約阿施
Joash, the Boy King

國王約阿施從小由叔叔耶何耶大帶大，
他登基成為國王後，很想修補聖殿，
可是人民很窮，約阿施用什麼方法來籌錢呢？

"Don't cry, little Joash, don't cry.
Someday you will be king
 and wear a crown on your head
 and sit on a golden throne.
But if the wicked queen hears you cry
 she will send her soldiers to take you away.
And then you won't be king
 and wear a crown on your head
 and sit on a golden throne."

「別哭，小約阿施，別哭！
有一天你將成為國王，
　頭上戴著皇冠，
　坐在黃金寶座上。
但是，如果邪惡的皇后聽到你的哭聲，
　她會派士兵來把你抓走。
這樣你就不能作國王了，
　也不能頭戴著皇冠，
　坐在黃金寶座上了。」

292

Uncle Jehoiada, who was priest of the Temple,
and Aunt Jehosheba kept baby Joash
in the bedroom of their Temple rooms.
Joash learned to walk; he learned to talk.
The wicked queen did not find him.

耶何耶大叔叔是聖殿的祭司，
　他和約示巴嬸嬸將嬰兒約阿施
　藏在他們聖殿的一間臥室裏。
漸漸的，約阿施學會了走路和講話，
還好壞皇后沒有找到他。

294

The boy Joash grew. Each birthday he stood
     a little taller beside the bedroom doorpost.
In the daytime, the door was always barred shut,
     lest someone in the Temple see him
     and go tell the wicked queen.
In the evening, when the people had gone home
     the door was unbarred, and Joash
     could walk with his uncle in the Temple court.

嬰兒約阿施長大了。每一年的生日，
他都站在臥房門柱的旁邊量身高，他一年比一年更高了，
白天的時候，臥室的門總是緊閉著，
     免得聖殿裏有人看見他，
     去向壞皇后報告。
到了晚上，當大家回家之後，
     房門的門閂就會打開，
     約阿施就可以和叔叔在聖殿的庭院裏散步。

Berran

One evening, as Joash and Uncle Jehoiada
    walked together in the Temple court,
    Joash saw a hole in the Temple wall;
    then he saw another hole, and another—
    why, the Temple walls were full of holes!
"The holes were made by the wicked queen's sons
    when they tore away parts of the walls to build
    a temple for their idol," said Uncle Jehoiada.
"To repair the holes would cost much money,
    and there is no money in the Temple treasury."

有一天晚上，當約阿施和耶何耶大叔叔
    一起在聖殿的庭院裏散步時，
    約阿施看見聖殿的牆上有一個洞，
    沒多久，他看見另一個洞，之後又有一個洞—
    怎麼回事！聖殿的牆上怎麼全都是洞啊！
「那些洞都是壞皇后的兒子們挖的，
    他們拆了部分的牆，
    拿去為他們的偶像蓋一座廟。」耶何耶大叔叔說。
「修補這些洞得花很多錢，
    可是聖殿的財庫已經沒有錢了。」

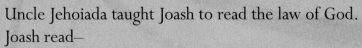

Uncle Jehoiada taught Joash to read the law of God.
Joash read—

"Thou shalt have no other gods before me...
Remenber the Sabbath day, to keep it holy...
Honour thy father and thy mother...
Thou shalt not steal."

Joash loved to read the law of God; he loved God.

耶何耶大叔叔教導約阿施閱讀上帝的律法。
約阿施朗誦著——

「除我以外，不可敬拜別的神……

要謹守安息日為聖日……

要孝敬父母……

不可偷竊。」

約阿施很喜愛閱讀上帝的律法；他愛上帝。

Then came the day that Joash was seven.
Uncle Jehoiada took him by the hand,
led him out on the Temple porch,
and stood him beside the bronze pillar.
Below the porch, to one side,
were singers, on the other,
trumpeters with silver trumpets.
Rows of soldiers with spears guarded the porch.
Many people were in the Temple court.
Quietly they watched and waited.

301

到了約阿施滿七歲的那一天，
耶何耶大叔叔牽著他的手，
　　帶他來到聖殿的門廊，
　　讓他站在銅柱旁邊。
在門廊下的這一邊，
　　有許多唱歌的人，而另一邊，
　　有許多號手拿著銀號角。
佩帶長矛的士兵列隊守著門廊。
好多人站在聖殿的庭院裏，
　　他們靜靜地圍觀和等待。

303

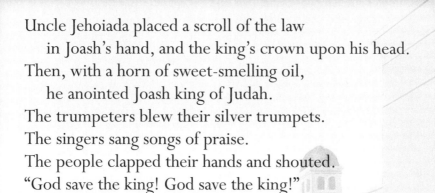

Uncle Jehoiada placed a scroll of the law
    in Joash's hand, and the king's crown upon his head.
Then, with a horn of sweet-smelling oil,
    he anointed Joash king of Judah.
The trumpeters blew their silver trumpets.
The singers sang songs of praise.
The people clapped their hands and shouted.
"God save the king! God save the king!"

耶何耶大叔叔把律法書的卷軸交在約阿施手裏，
    將皇冠戴在他的頭上。
接著，他用牛角裝著香膏油，
    將油膏在約阿施的頭上，封他為猶大國的國王。
號手們吹奏起了他們的銀號角。
歌手們也唱起了讚美的詩歌。
人們鼓掌歡呼。
「神佑吾王！神佑吾王！」

305

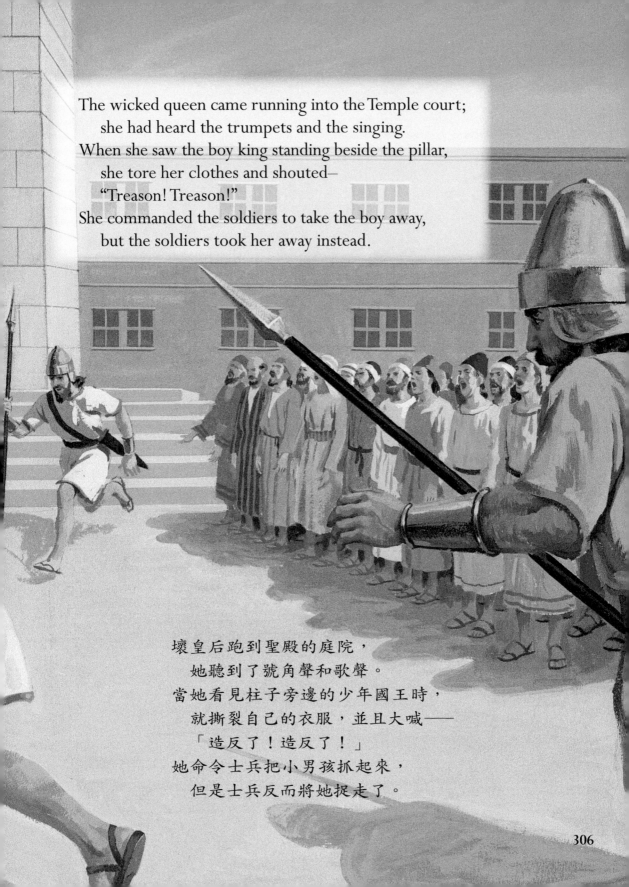

The wicked queen came running into the Temple court;
    she had heard the trumpets and the singing.
When she saw the boy king standing beside the pillar,
    she tore her clothes and shouted–
    "Treason! Treason!"
She commanded the soldiers to take the boy away,
    but the soldiers took her away instead.

壞皇后跑到聖殿的庭院，
    她聽到了號角聲和歌聲。
當她看見柱子旁邊的少年國王時，
    就撕裂自己的衣服，並且大喊——
    「造反了！造反了！」
她命令士兵把小男孩抓起來，
    但是士兵反而將她捉走了。

The people lined up in a long procession,
	soldiers, singers, and priests;
	the trumpeters led the way.
Out of the Temple gate,
	and down the street to the king's palace,
	they carried the boy king, Joash.
This palace would now be his home.

眾人排成一列長長的隊伍，
　有士兵、歌手、祭司，
　號手們領隊前進。
他們抬著小國王約阿施。
　走出聖殿的大門，
　走向國王的皇宮，
從此以後，這座皇宮就是他的家了。

Slowly, Joash walked up the palace aisle.
He climbed the steps to the golden throne.
The throne was very large
    and his feet did not reach the floor,
    but he sat as straight as a king.
Again the trumpeters blew their trumpets;
    the singers sang; and the people shouted,
"God save the king! God save the king!"

309

Berran

慢慢地，約阿施走向宮殿的走道。
他踏上階梯，來到黃金寶座前面。
寶座非常高大，
　　他的腳搆不到地面，
　　但是，他直挺挺地坐著，顯出國王的樣子。
號手們又吹奏起他們的號角；
　　歌手們也唱起了歌；人們一起跟著歡呼：
「神佑吾王！神佑吾王！」

To be king was a big task for a boy; he would need
  Uncle Jehoiada's help for many years.
King Joash remembered the holes in the Temple wall.
How could he get the money to mend them?
He sent men throughout the land to collect coins,
  but the men spent the coins on their own houses.
The holes in the Temple walls were still there.
Then Joash thought of a different plan to raise money.

Berran

對一位少年來說，作國王是一件艱辛的事；
幾年之內，他都需要耶何耶大叔叔的幫忙。
約阿施王記得聖殿牆上的那些破洞。
他要怎樣籌到錢去修補那些破洞呢？
他派人到全國各地去募款，
但是，人們都把錢用來修繕自己的房子了。
聖殿牆上的破洞仍然在那裏。
約阿施想到一個很不一樣的方法來籌款。

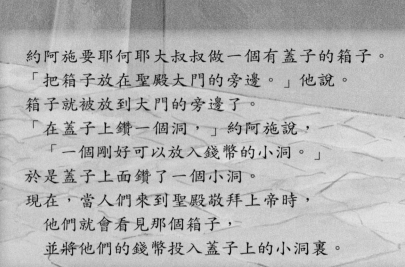

Joash asked Uncle Jehoiada for a chest with a lid.

"Let us put the chest beside the Temple gate," he said.

The chest was placed beside the gate.

"Let us cut a hole in the lid," said Joash,

"a hole just large enough for coins to go through."

The hole was cut in the lid.

Now, when people came to the Temple to worship,

they would see the chest,

and drop coins through the hole in its lid.

約阿施要耶何耶大叔叔做一個有蓋子的箱子。

「把箱子放在聖殿大門的旁邊。」他說。

箱子就被放到大門的旁邊了。

「在蓋子上鑽一個洞，」約阿施說，

「一個剛好可以放入錢幣的小洞。」

於是蓋子上面鑽了一個小洞。

現在，當人們來到聖殿敬拜上帝時，

他們就會看見那個箱子，

並將他們的錢幣投入蓋子上的小洞裏。

Berran

People came from near and far
to see the king's money chest.
Boys and girls came, fathers and mothers,
grandfathers and grandmothers.
They marched by and dropped coins into the chest.
At first, the coins made a *clinkety, clink, clink* sound.
When the chest was half filled,
clankety, clank, clank;
and when it was almost full, just *clunk*.

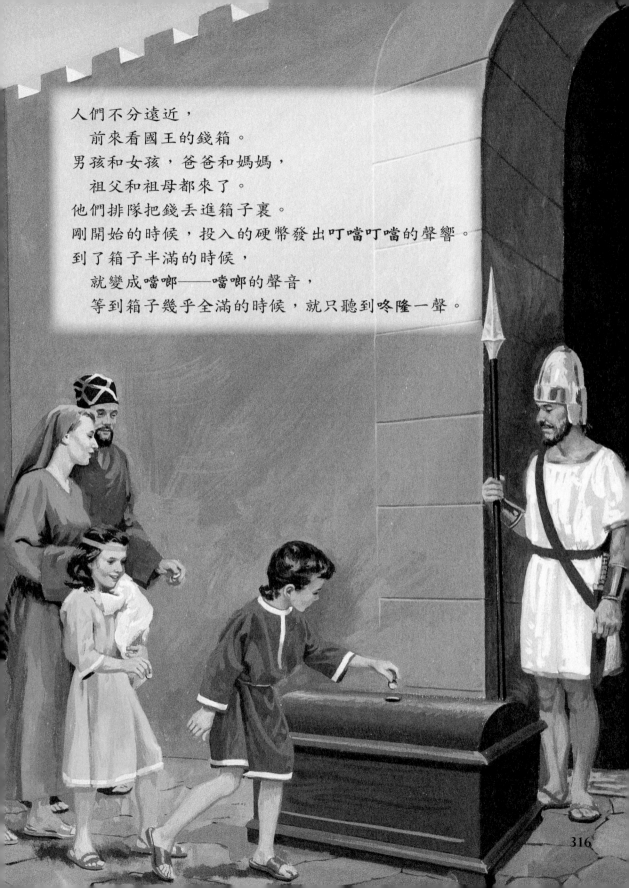

人們不分遠近，
　　前來看國王的錢箱。
男孩和女孩，爸爸和媽媽，
　　祖父和祖母都來了。
他們排隊把錢丟進箱子裏。
剛開始的時候，投入的硬幣發出叮噹叮噹的聲響。
到了箱子半滿的時候，
　　就變成噹啷——噹啷的聲音，
　　等到箱子幾乎全滿的時候，就只聽到咚隆一聲。

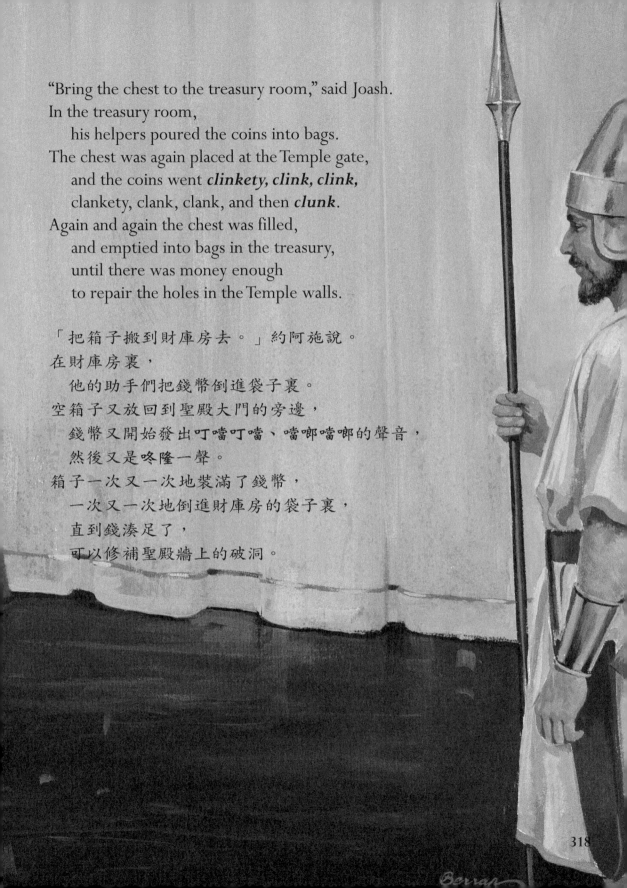

"Bring the chest to the treasury room," said Joash.
In the treasury room,
    his helpers poured the coins into bags.
The chest was again placed at the Temple gate,
    and the coins went *clinkety, clink, clink,*
    clankety, clank, clank, and then *clunk*.
Again and again the chest was filled,
    and emptied into bags in the treasury,
    until there was money enough
    to repair the holes in the Temple walls.

「把箱子搬到財庫房去。」約阿施說。
在財庫房裏，
    他的助手們把錢幣倒進袋子裏。
空箱子又放回到聖殿大門的旁邊，
    錢幣又開始發出叮噹叮噹、噹啷噹啷的聲音，
    然後又是咚隆一聲。
箱子一次又一次地裝滿了錢幣，
    一次又一次地倒進財庫房的袋子裏，
    直到錢湊足了，
    可以修補聖殿牆上的破洞。

Stonecutters cut stones, carpenters sawed boards.
Carefully they worked, for this was God's house.
At last, the holes in the Temple walls were repaired.
Now, many people came to worship in the Temple.
They learned to love God as did Joash, their king.
God looked down from heaven
and was pleased to see
the beautiful Temple,
the worshiping people,
and the young king
on the golden throne.

石匠們磨著石頭，木匠們也鋸著木板。

他們小心翼翼地工作，因為這是上帝的房子。

最後，聖殿牆上所有的破洞都補好了。

現在，許多人會來到聖殿敬拜上帝。

他們學會了愛上帝，就像他們的國王約阿施一樣。

上帝從天上向下俯視，

　他很高興地看著地上，

　美麗的聖殿，

　敬拜的人們，

　以及坐在黃金寶座上的年輕國王。

上帝洗淨大地
When God Washed the World

上帝發現祂所造的世界變得好邪惡，
只剩下挪亞一家是好人。
上帝要降下大洪水來洗淨邪惡，
於是挪亞造了一艘方舟，但是大洪水真的會來嗎？

In the beginning—
    when God looked at the earth He had made,
        behold, it was good, very good.
The people were good, the animals were tame,
    the birds were not afraid.
God was pleased with what He saw.

起初——

　　上帝看著祂所創造的這個地球，

　　看啊！這地球多美好，多麼美好啊！

人們很善良，動物很溫馴，

　　鳥兒也不會覺得害怕。

上帝看著這一切，感到十分滿意。

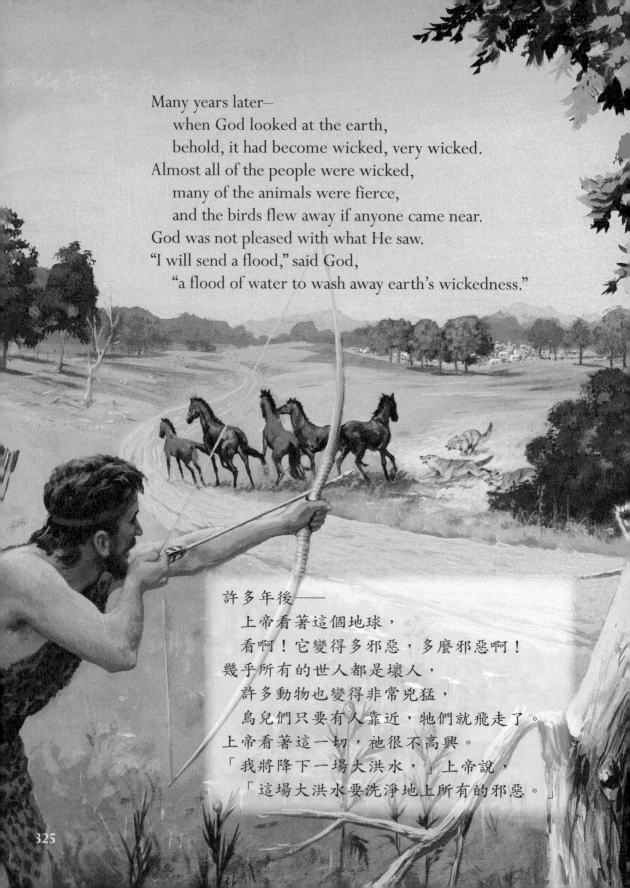

Many years later—
    when God looked at the earth,
        behold, it had become wicked, very wicked.
Almost all of the people were wicked,
    many of the animals were fierce,
        and the birds flew away if anyone came near.
God was not pleased with what He saw.
"I will send a flood," said God,
    "a flood of water to wash away earth's wickedness."

許多年後──
    上帝看著這個地球，
    看啊！它變得多邪惡，多麼邪惡啊！
幾乎所有的世人都是壞人，
    許多動物也變得非常兇猛，
    鳥兒們只要有人靠近，牠們就飛走了。
上帝看著這一切，祂很不高興。
「我將降下一場大洪水，」上帝說，
    「這場大洪水要洗淨地上所有的邪惡。」

326

In a green valley near a cypress forest
    lived the good man Noah with his good wife.
Every morning and evening Noah talked with God.
God told Noah about the flood He was sending
    to wash away earth's wickedness.
The water would be so deep—
    it would cover the cypress trees,
    it would cover the highest mountains.
Said God to Noah,
    "Build an ark for the saving of all that will come into it."

在柏木樹林附近，有一個綠意盎然的山谷，
    住著一對好人，挪亞和他的妻子。
每天早晚，挪亞都和上帝說話。
上帝告訴挪亞，祂要降下一場大洪水，
    洗去大地的邪惡。
大洪水將會淹到這麼深——
    它會淹過柏木樹林，
    它會淹過最高的山。
上帝對挪亞說：
    「造一艘方舟，拯救那些願意進去方舟的生物。」

Berron

God told Noah just how to build the ark.
"Build it long, build it wide," said God,
    "build it three stories high.
Make a window in the roof, and a door in the side.
            Make rooms for people,
                rooms for animals,
                rooms for birds,
                and rooms for food.
            Build it of cypress wood,
                and daub it with pitch within
                and without."
            Noah drew a picture of the ark;
                it looked like a ship below,
                and a house above.

上帝告訴挪亞如何建造方舟。
「把它造得又長又寬，」上帝說，
　「要有三層樓那麼高，
船頂上造一扇天窗，旁邊還要造一扇門。
要有房間讓人們住，
　要有房間安置動物，
　要有房間留給鳥兒，
　要有房間儲存食物。
要用柏木打造方舟，
　　裏裏外外都要塗上松香。」
挪亞畫了一張方舟的圖畫；
　它看起來下面像一艘船，
　上面像一棟房屋。

330

Noah hired workmen with sharp axes and saws
　　to go into the cypress forest to cut down trees.
From the forest came the sound of chopping and sawing,
　　and great trees falling.
When a giant cypress fell, the ground shook.
Bullocks dragged the logs into the green valley.
There, men sawed them into beams and boards
　　for the building of the ark.

挪亞僱用了工人，要他們帶著鋒利的斧頭和鋸子
　　到柏木林裏去砍樹。
樹林裏傳來了砍樹和鋸木頭的聲音，
　　以及大樹倒地的聲音。
每當大柏樹倒下時，大地就會震動，
公牛把木頭拉到綠油油的山谷裏，
在山谷裏，人們將木頭鋸成橫樑和木板，
　　準備用來蓋方舟。

During the time of cutting trees and building the ark,
    three sons were born to Noah and his wife.
They named the oldest son Japheth,
    the middle son Shem, and the youngest son Ham.
As the boys were growing,
    there were many things they could do to help their father.
They could be water boys and carry water.
They could gather pitch to daub the ark.
They could ride and guide the bullocks.

在建造方舟的期間，
　　挪亞的妻子陸續生了三個兒子。
最大的兒子叫雅弗。
　　二兒子叫閃，小兒子叫含。
這三個男孩長大了，
　　他們可以幫忙爸爸做許多事。
他們可以幫忙送水和挑水。
他們可以收集松香，塗在方舟上。
他們可以騎著公牛，指引牠們的方向。

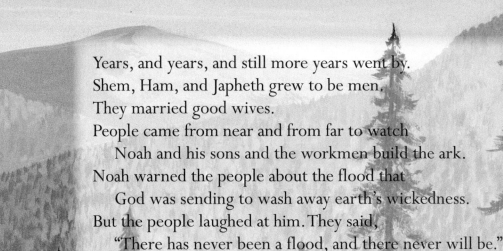

Years, and years, and still more years went by.
Shem, Ham, and Japheth grew to be men.
They married good wives.
People came from near and from far to watch
    Noah and his sons and the workmen build the ark.
Noah warned the people about the flood that
    God was sending to wash away earth's wickedness.
But the people laughed at him. They said,
    "There has never been a flood, and there never will be."

年復一年，好多年過去。
閃、含和雅弗都長大成人了。
他們也娶了好妻子。
　　　　　人們不分遠近都跑來看挪亞和他的兒子們，
　　　　　　　以及工人們所建造的那艘方舟。
　　　　　　挪亞警告大家，上帝會降下洪水，
　　　　　　　　來洗淨大地的邪惡。
　　　　　　　但是大家都嘲笑他。
　　　　　　　他們說：「從來沒有
　　　　　　　發生過大洪水，
　　　　　　　將來也不會有。」

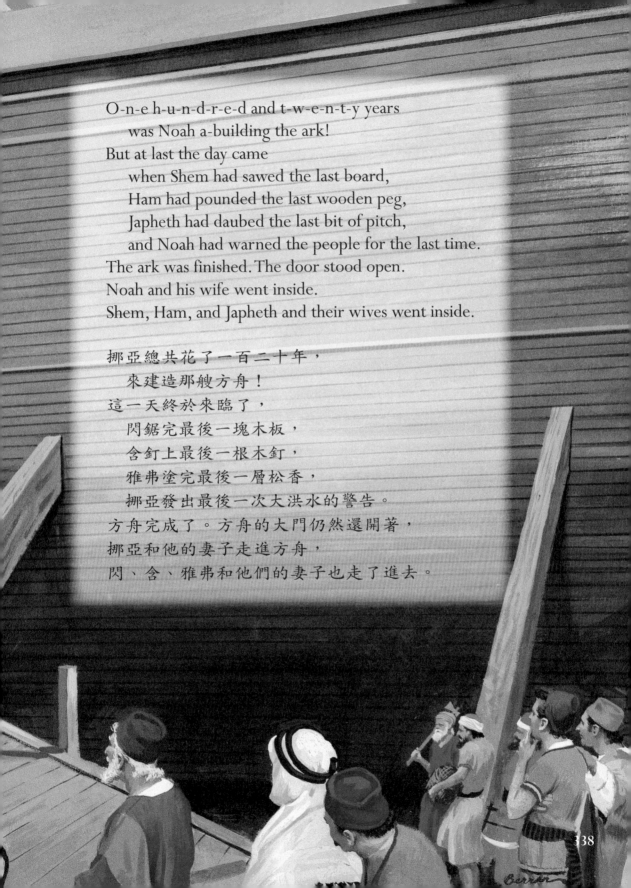

O-n-e h-u-n-d-r-e-d and t-w-e-n-t-y years
　　was Noah a-building the ark!
But at last the day came
　　when Shem had sawed the last board,
　　Ham had pounded the last wooden peg,
　　Japheth had daubed the last bit of pitch,
　　and Noah had warned the people for the last time.
The ark was finished. The door stood open.
Noah and his wife went inside.
Shem, Ham, and Japheth and their wives went inside.

挪亞總共花了一百二十年，
　　來建造那艘方舟！
這一天終於來臨了，
　　閃鋸完最後一塊木板，
　　含釘上最後一根木釘，
　　雅弗塗完最後一層松香，
　　挪亞發出最後一次大洪水的警告。
方舟完成了。方舟的大門仍然還開著，
挪亞和他的妻子走進方舟，
閃、含、雅弗和他們的妻子也走了進去。

The people outside the ark laughed and laughed.
"Ho! Ho! Ho!" they said,
   "Where is the water to float your ark?
   Who said there would be a flood?
   It has never rained. It never will."
Then someone on the edge of the crowd pointed toward the forest.
"Look–look at the animals!"

站在方舟外面的群眾不斷嘲笑他們。

「哈！哈！哈！」他們說，

「哪裏有水可以讓你們的方舟浮起來呀？

誰說會有大洪水呀？

以前從來沒有下過雨，以後也不會下雨。」

沒多久，群眾的最外圍有一個小孩指著森林。

「你們快看！你們快看那些動物！」

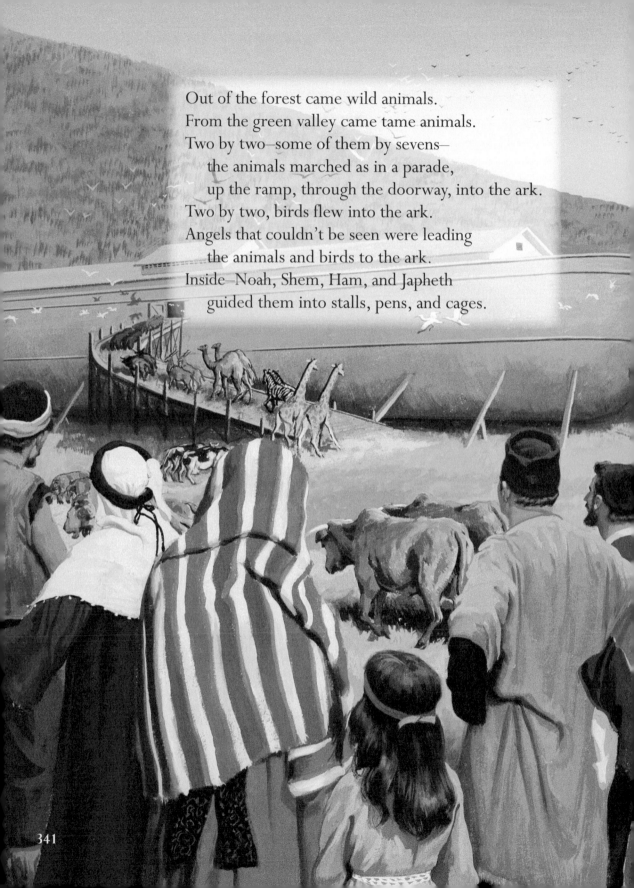

Out of the forest came wild animals.
From the green valley came tame animals.
Two by two—some of them by sevens—
   the animals marched as in a parade,
   up the ramp, through the doorway, into the ark.
Two by two, birds flew into the ark.
Angels that couldn't be seen were leading
   the animals and birds to the ark.
Inside—Noah, Shem, Ham, and Japheth
   guided them into stalls, pens, and cages.

一群野生動物從森林裏走出來。
馴養的動物從翠綠的山谷裏走出來。
牠們成雙成對──有的是七公七母──
　　這些動物一齊邁步前進，好像在遊行，
　　牠們走上斜坡，經過門口，進入方舟。
鳥兒也成雙成對地飛進方舟，
　　看不見的天使領著動物和飛鳥進入方舟。
在方舟裏面，有挪亞、閃、含、雅弗
　　引導牠們進入廄房、畜舍、籠子裏。

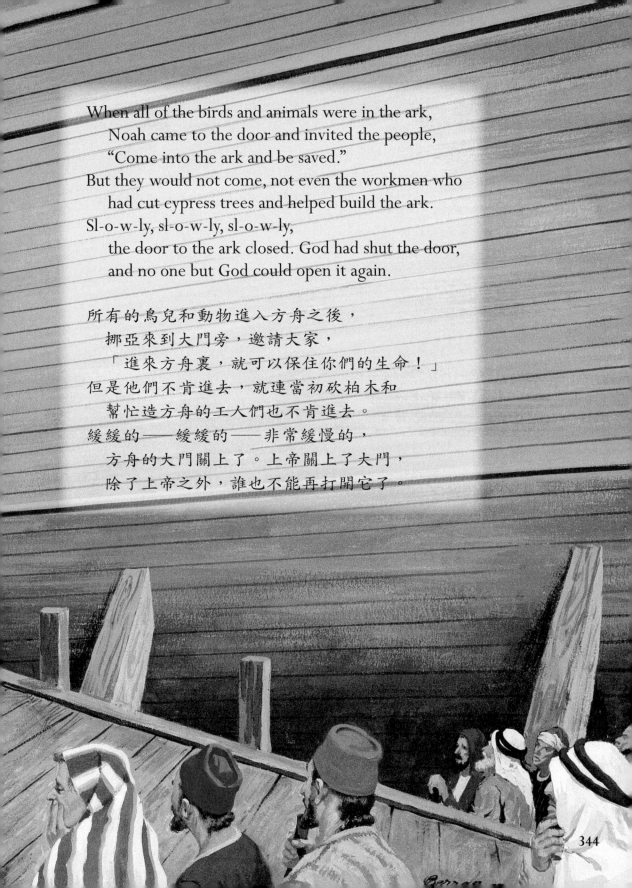

When all of the birds and animals were in the ark,
    Noah came to the door and invited the people,
    "Come into the ark and be saved."
But they would not come, not even the workmen who
    had cut cypress trees and helped build the ark.
Sl-o-w-ly, sl-o-w-ly, sl-o-w-ly,
    the door to the ark closed. God had shut the door,
    and no one but God could open it again.

所有的鳥兒和動物進入方舟之後，
    挪亞來到大門旁，邀請大家，
    「進來方舟裏，就可以保住你們的生命！」
但是他們不肯進去，就連當初砍柏木和
    幫忙造方舟的工人們也不肯進去。
緩緩的——緩緩的——非常緩慢的，
    方舟的大門關上了。上帝關上了大門，
    除了上帝之外，誰也不能再打開它了。

Inside the ark, Noah and his wife,
and Shem, Ham, and Japheth with their wives
waited and listened—listened and waited.
But nothing happened that day,
nor the next, nor the next, nor the next.
Seven days Noah and his family
waited and listened—listened and waited,
and then they heard it...

在方舟裏，挪亞和他的妻子，
　　還有閃、含、雅弗和他們的妻子，
　　他們等待，傾聽——傾聽，等待。
但是什麼事也沒發生，
　　第二天，第三天，第四天也是一樣。
挪亞和家人已經等了七天了，
　　他們還在等待，傾聽——傾聽，等待。
　　最後，他們似乎聽見了……

"Splat, splatter, splash!" Rain fell on the ark.
"Splat, splatter, splash, pour!" It rained harder.
Noah looked up through the ark window.
He saw angry clouds; he saw lightning.
He heard the thunder roll and the wind roar.
"Flash! Crash! Roar! Pour!"
The animals were frightened.
Cows bawled! Tigers screamed! Elephants trumpeted!
But Noah and his family were not afraid.
They knew God would take care of them.

「滴滴答答！滴滴答答」小雨點開始落在方舟上。
「淅瀝淅瀝！嘩啦嘩啦！」雨越下越大了。
挪亞往上面的窗戶望過去。
他看見狂暴的烏雲，他看見閃電。
他聽見雷聲隆隆作響，還有狂風呼嘯聲。
「唰！轟隆！吼！嘩啦！」
動物們都嚇壞了。
牛隻放聲大叫！老虎拼命嘶吼！大象仰天呼嘯！
但是挪亞和他的家人並不害怕，
他們知道上帝會照顧他們。

349

The water became deeper, and deeper, and deeper,
　　until it was a sea of tumbling waves.
The ark rode the waves up; it rode the waves down.
It tipped this way; it tipped that way.
But it was made of strong cypress wood,
　　and made after God's plan.
Noah, Shem, Ham, and Japheth had built it well.
Day and night, angels watched over the ark.
Safely it rode through the storm.

水位變深了，水越漲越高，
　　雨水最後變成波浪洶湧的海洋。
方舟乘風破浪，又上又下。
它一下偏向這邊，一下又傾向那邊。
但是方舟是用堅固的柏木造成的，
　　它是根據上帝的設計所造成的。
挪亞、閃、含和雅弗將方舟打造得非常堅固。
不管白日晚上，都有天使們看顧著這艘方舟。
它安全地度過暴風雨的襲擊。

Forty days, forty nights, it rained, and then the rain stopped.
The ark floated quietly on the water.
The animals and birds became less afraid.
When Noah, Shem, Ham, and Japheth fed them,
    the animals made eager sniffs and snuffs,
    monkeys chattered, birds twittered.
One day Noah felt the bottom of the ark
    scrape on the ground. Then it stood still.
"The water must be going down," he said.

雨下了整整四十天、四十夜，最後雨終於停了。
方舟靜靜地漂浮在水面上。
動物和鳥兒漸漸不再感到害怕了。
挪亞、閃、含和雅弗餵食物給牠們吃的時候，
　　動物們使勁的又聞又嗅，
　　猴子吱吱喳喳的叫，
　　鳥兒也喊喊喳喳的喞啾。
有一天，挪亞感覺方舟的
　　船底刮過地面，接著船靜止不動了。
「一定是大洪水退了。」他說。

"I will let a bird fly out the window," said Noah.
"If the water has gone down below the treetops,
   the bird will stay in the trees and not return."
Noah first sent out Black Raven,
   and later White Dove,
   but they both came back to the ark.
Noah said, "The water still covers the trees."
Then one day White Dove brought back an olive leaf,
   and another day, she didn't come back at all.
"The water is drying up," said Noah.

「我放一隻鳥兒飛出去看看，」挪亞說，
「如果水位已經退得比樹梢還低，
　鳥兒就會待在樹梢上，不會再回來了。」
挪亞先放出一隻烏鴉，
　然後是一隻白鴿，
　但是牠們都飛回來了。
挪亞說：「洪水還是淹過樹木。」
有一天，白鴿叼了一片橄欖葉回來，
　又有一天，牠不再飛回來了。
「看來水快要乾了，」挪亞說。

Days and days, and more days went by...
and it was Noah's birthday.
He was six hundred and one years old.
Noah, Shem, Ham, and Japheth made the day special
by removing the roof of the ark.
They looked out and saw that the ark rested
high up in the mountains. They saw trees
that were uprooted, and rocks tumbled about,
but the ground was dry, and grass was growing.
Still, God did not open the door of the ark—
not yet.

一天又一天，一天又一天地過去了……
　這一天是挪亞的生日。
他已經六百零一歲了。
在這個特別的日子，挪亞、閃、含和雅弗
　把方舟的頂端打開來。
他們往外望，看到方舟停在一座高山的山頂上。
　他們看見樹木被連根拔起，
　岩石到處崩塌散落，
　但是大地已經乾了，小草也長出來了。
然而，上帝仍然沒有把方舟的門打開——
　時候還未到。

One day, after the grass had grown tall enough
　　to give the animals plenty of food,
　　slowly, slowly, the door of the ark opened.
Noah opened the doors of the rooms inside,
　　and the animals came hurrying out of the ark.
They barked, they trumpeted, they squealed for joy.
They rolled over and over in the cool green grass,
　　and then raced down the mountainside.
Songbirds sang, "God is good, God is love,"
　　then flew away to find places to build their nests.

這一天，綠草已經長得非常高了，
　足夠成為動物們的食物，
　慢慢地，慢慢地，方舟的大門打開了。
挪亞打開船上所有房間的門，
　動物急忙跑到方舟外面。
牠們高興地吠叫，高呼，長嘯。
牠們在翠綠涼爽的草地上翻滾，
　然後快步衝下山去。
唱歌的小鳥高唱：「上帝多美好，上帝就是愛。」
　接著，牠們飛走了，牠們要去找地方築巢了。

Noah, Shem, Ham, and Japheth gathered stones
and built an altar unto the Lord.
The family knelt about the altar
while Noah prayed,
"Thank you, God, for keeping us safe.
Thank you for the good clean earth."
God answered by hanging
a rainbow in the sky,
the very first rainbow ever to be seen.
He said, *"I do set my bow in the cloud,
and it shall be for a token that the water
shall no more cover the whole earth."*

挪亞、閃、含和雅弗聚集一堆石頭，
為上帝搭建了一座祭壇。
一家人圍著祭壇跪下，然後挪亞開口禱告：
「謝謝你，上帝，保守我們一切平安。
謝謝你將大地清洗的如此乾淨。」
上帝在天空中掛上一道彩虹作為回應，
那是世上有始以來出現的第一道彩虹。
祂說：「我使彩虹在雲端出現，
作為立約的記號，
約定不再用洪水毀滅地上所有的生物。」

但以理和獅子
Daniel and the Lions

巴比倫國王讓聰明的但以理幫他管理國家，
可是那些總督們很不服氣，
一心想找出但以理的把柄，
於是，他們想出了一個狡猾的計謀來陷害但以理……

Many years had gone by since Daniel
    had been taken a prisoner to Babylon.
He had grown to be a wise, good man.
And now a new king sat upon the royal throne.
The new king soon learned that no matter what
    happened, he could trust Daniel.
So the new king made Daniel ruler next to himself:
    over all the people of the kingdom,
    over all the wise men of the kingdom,
    over all the princes of the kingdom.

自從但以理被俘虜到巴比倫之後，
    已經過了好多年。
他長成一位有智慧又善良的人。
現在新國王登基了。
新國王很快就學會，不論發生什麼事，
    他都能信靠但以理。
所以，新國王讓但以理來管理在他之下的人：
    國內所有的百姓，
    國內所有的智者，
    國內所有的總督。

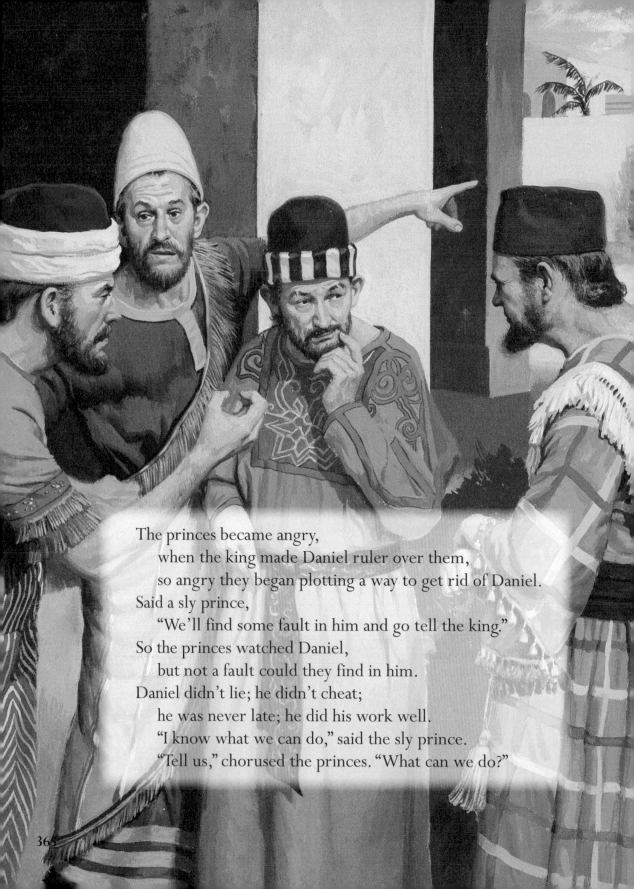

The princes became angry,
    when the king made Daniel ruler over them,
    so angry they began plotting a way to get rid of Daniel.
Said a sly prince,
    "We'll find some fault in him and go tell the king."
So the princes watched Daniel,
    but not a fault could they find in him.
Daniel didn't lie; he didn't cheat;
    he was never late; he did his work well.
    "I know what we can do," said the sly prince.
    "Tell us," chorused the princes. "What can we do?"

總督們很生氣，
　　因為國王竟任命但以理來管理他們，
　　他們憤怒到想找出一個辦法，來除掉但以理。
一名狡猾的總督說：
　　「我們可以找出他的把柄，然後向國王稟報。」
所以總督們隨時監視著但以理，
　　可是他們在但以理身上找不到任何把柄。
但以理不說謊、不欺騙；
　　他也從不遲到；他總是把工作做得很好。
　　「我知道我們可以怎麼做了！」那名狡猾的總督說。
　　「快告訴我們！」總督們異口同聲地說。
　　「我們可以怎麼做？」

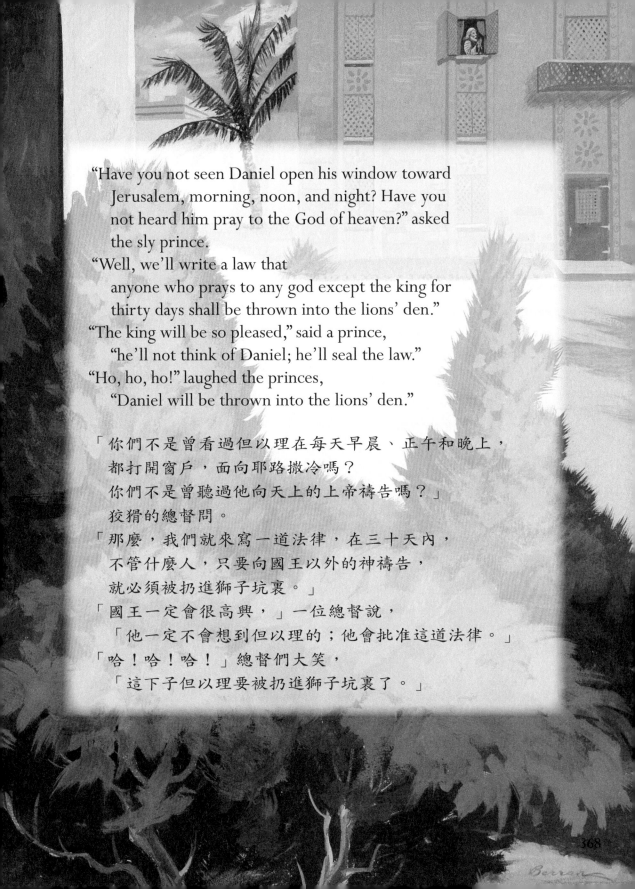

"Have you not seen Daniel open his window toward
  Jerusalem, morning, noon, and night? Have you
  not heard him pray to the God of heaven?" asked
  the sly prince.
"Well, we'll write a law that
  anyone who prays to any god except the king for
  thirty days shall be thrown into the lions' den."
"The king will be so pleased," said a prince,
  "he'll not think of Daniel; he'll seal the law."
"Ho, ho, ho!" laughed the princes,
  "Daniel will be thrown into the lions' den."

「你們不是曾看過但以理在每天早晨、正午和晚上，
  都打開窗戶，面向耶路撒冷嗎？
  你們不是曾聽過他向天上的上帝禱告嗎？」
  狡猾的總督問。
「那麼，我們就來寫一道法律，在三十天內，
  不管什麼人，只要向國王以外的神禱告，
  就必須被扔進獅子坑裏。」
「國王一定會很高興，」一位總督說，
  「他一定不會想到但以理的；他會批准這道法律。」
「哈！哈！哈！」總督們大笑，
  「這下子但以理要被扔進獅子坑裏了。」

The princes wrote the law and took it to the king.
"O king, we wish to honor you," said the sly one.
"We have written a law that anyone who prays to
any god except you. O king, for thirty days,
he shall be thrown into the lions' den."

The king was pleased; he asked for wax
that he might seal the law.
A servant dripped melted wax on the paper.
The king pressed his ring into it; and so
the law was sealed; it could not be changed.

總督們寫下這道禁令後，將它拿給國王看。

「王啊，我們希望能榮耀您的名，」那名狡猾的總督說，

「我們寫下了一道禁令，在三十天內，不管什麼人，

　　只要向國王以外的神禱告，

　　就必須被扔進獅子坑裏。」

國王很高興；他叫人遞上蠟，

　　好讓他為這道禁令蓋上印。

一名僕人在禁令的紙上滴下融化的蠟油，

國王在紙上蓋下他的指印；

　　這道禁令蓋上印後，就不能再更改了。

Messengers were stationed on the city streets
      To read the new law to the people.
"Hear ye! Hear ye!" shouted the messengers.
"He who prays to any god
      other than the king for thirty days
      shall be thrown into the lions' den."
Fathers and mothers stopped to listen;
      boys and girls stopped to listen;
      Daniel stopped to listen to the reading
      of the strange new law.

信差們被派到街頭巷尾，
　向百姓宣讀這道禁令。
「注意聽！注意聽！」信差大聲宣讀，
　「在三十天內，不管什麼人，
　只要向國王以外的神禱告，
　就必須被扔進獅子坑裏。」
爸爸和媽媽停下來聆聽；
　男孩和女孩停下來注意聽；
　但以理也停下來聽他們宣讀
　這道奇怪的新法律。

Several of the princes hurried down the street
    that led to Daniel's house.
They hid where they could see the window
    that he always opened when he prayed.
They saw Daniel come home and go into the house.
Would Daniel open his window and pray as always?
Perhaps he would pray in his closet today.
Maybe he wouldn't pray at all
    until the thirty days were past.
Anxiously the princes watched and waited.
And then…

好幾名總督急忙趕到那條
　　通往但以理家的街道。
他們躲在可以偷看到那扇窗戶的地方，
　　因為但以理禱告的時候，總是打開那扇窗戶。
他們看見但以理回家，進入屋子裏。
但以理會不會像往常一樣，打開他的窗戶禱告呢？
或許他今天會在他的內室裏禱告。
或許他根本就不禱告，
　　直到三十天過去。
總督們焦急地觀察和等待。
不久……

Daniel's window opened wide.
The princes saw Daniel kneel in the open window;
    they heard him pray to the God of heaven.
They didn't wait for Daniel to say Amen.
They raced to tell the other princes
    what they had seen and heard.
Together they would go tell the king.
Their plan had worked. Daniel would be thrown
    into the lions' den. They would be rid of him.

但以理的窗戶打開了。
總督們看見但以理跪在敞開的窗戶前面；
　　他們聽見他向天上的上帝禱告。
他們還沒有等到但以理禱告結束，說「阿們」，
　　就急忙跑去把所見所聞告訴其他的總督們。
他們要一起去向國王稟報。
他們的計謀總算得逞了。但以理要被扔進獅子坑裏。
　　他們終於可以除掉他了。

The king was sad, so sad for his friend Daniel.
He was very sorry that he had sealed the law.
Guards brought Daniel to the lions' den.
Other guards rolled away the stone
   from the opening to the den.
The lions were hungry; they growled;
   they roared so loudly the ground trembled.
One guard seized Daniel's arms,
   another his feet; they threw him down
   among the roaring lions,
   and then rolled the stone
   back in place.

國王很傷心，為他的朋友但以理傷心。
他非常後悔為那道禁令蓋上印。
守衛們把但以理帶到獅子坑的前面。
其他的守衛將洞口的石頭挪開。
獅子都很飢餓；牠們咆哮著；
　　牠們大聲怒吼，甚至連地面都在震動。
一名守衛抓住但以理的雙臂，
　　另一名守衛抓住他的雙腳；
　　他們把但以理扔進怒吼的獅子群中，
　　再將石頭滾回原處。

Suddenly, everything became quiet;
    the lions no longer roared;
    the ground no longer trembled.
The proud princes smiled at one another;
    they were rid of Daniel; they were sure
    they would never see him again.
But the king wept.

突然間，一切都平靜下來了；
　　獅子不再咆哮；
　　地面也不再震動。
總督們得意洋洋地露出笑容看著彼此，
　　他們除掉但以理了；他們相信，
　　從此以後，他們再也不會見到他了。
然而，國王卻哭了。

Day turned into night:
    the moon came up;
    hundreds and hundreds of stars
    sparkled in the dark night sky.
The king couldn't sleep. He refused to eat;
    he would allow no music to be played.
From time to time he listened toward the window.
Often on other nights the lions roared,
    but tonight the lions were quiet.

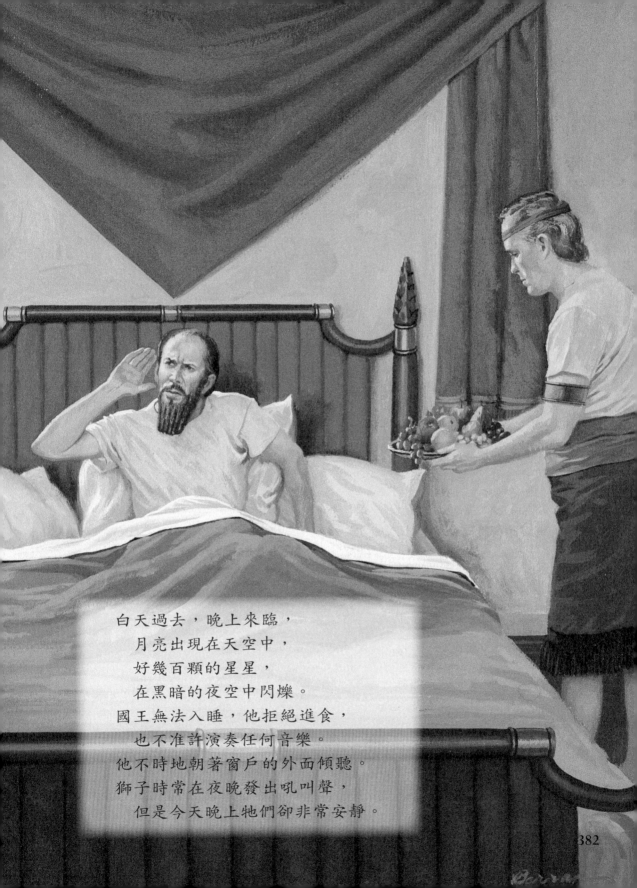

白天過去，晚上來臨，
　月亮出現在天空中，
　好幾百顆的星星，
　在黑暗的夜空中閃爍。
國王無法入睡，他拒絕進食，
　也不准許演奏任何音樂。
他不時地朝著窗戶的外面傾聽。
獅子時常在夜晚發出吼叫聲，
　但是今天晚上牠們卻非常安靜。

Next morning–
    as soon as the sky began to come light,
    the king sent for his guard
    and hurried to the lions' den.
The guard rolled away the heavy stone.
Anxiously the king called down into the den,
    "O Daniel,…is thy God, whom thou servest…
    able to deliver thee from the lions?"
Would Daniel answer? Was he still alive?

第二天清早——
    天剛亮的時候，
    國王就召喚守衛，
    並急忙趕往獅子坑。
守衛挪開沉重的石頭。
國王焦急地朝著坑內呼喚：
    「但以理啊！…你忠心事奉的上帝…
    能救你脫離獅子的口嗎？」
但以理會回答嗎？他還活著嗎？

From down in the lions' den
    came Daniel's quiet voice.
"O king, live for ever.
    My God hath sent His angel,
    and hath shut the lions' mouths,
    that they have not hurt me."

從獅子坑的深處，
　　傳來但以理平靜的聲音。
「國王萬歲！我的上帝差派天使，
　　封住了獅子的口，
　　使牠們不能傷害我。」

386

Joyously the king ordered the guard
    to take Daniel up out of the lions' den.
The guard let down a rope to Daniel.
Hardly was Daniel out of the den
    when the lions began to roar
    and the ground to tremble.
But there wasn't a tear in Daniel's clothes;
    there wasn't a claw mark on his hands;
    there wasn't a scratch on his face.

國王欣喜若狂，他好開心，
　他命令守衛將但以理從獅子坑裏拉上來。
守衛拋下繩索給但以理。
但以理才剛剛爬出獅子坑外，
　獅群就開始咆哮，
　地面也開始震動，
然而但以理的衣服絲毫沒有被撕裂的痕跡，
　他的手上也沒有任何的爪痕，
　甚至臉上也沒有任何被抓的傷痕。

Even as God sent an angel long ago
to shut the lions' mouths
to keep them from hurting Daniel,
just so He has promised to send an angel
today to protect everyone who loves Him.
In His Book God has written:
*"The angel of the Lord encampeth
round about them that fear love him,
and delivereth them."* Psalm 34:7.
Do you love Him?

上帝老早就差派一位天使，
去封住獅子的口，
使牠們無法傷害但以理，
同樣，今天上帝也承諾我們，祂會差派天使，
來保護每一個愛祂的人。
上帝在祂的《聖經》裏寫著：
「上主的天使保護敬畏（愛）祂的人，
救他們脫離危險。」（詩篇 34：7）
你愛祂嗎？

390

大麥餅與魚
Barley Loaves and Fishes

1 你曾經分享過你的食物給其他沒食物吃的同學嗎？

2 少年的籃子裏只有五塊餅和兩條魚，怎麼可以餵飽那麼多在場聽故事的群眾呢？

3 群眾聽完故事的時候，耶穌為什麼不直接叫大家回家吃飯呢？

4 如果你是這名少年，籃子裏有你最愛吃的食物，你還會不會把籃子拿出來分享？

少年國王約阿施
Joash, the Boy King

1 你覺得男孩約阿施的表現，可以成為一位受人尊敬的國王嗎？

2 約阿施的優點是什麼？

3 你認為耶和耶大是一位什麼樣的祭司？

4 如果教堂需要經費來修繕，你願意奉獻幫助嗎？

上帝洗淨大地
When God Washed the World

1. 上帝為何要用洪水毀滅地上的一切？
2. 上帝又為何只選上挪亞一家人為祂造方舟呢？
3. 為何那些動物會一對對或七隻七隻乖乖地進入方舟？
4. 彩虹出現代表什麼意義呢？

但以理和獅子
Daniel and the Lions

1. 你認為但以理從俘虜的身分到深受巴比倫國王寵愛的原因有哪些？
2. 為何其他的總督們想要陷害但以理？
3. 但以理被陷害丟進獅子坑裏的原因是什麼？他在坑裏發生了什麼事？

Crossword Puzzles

Part1

請參閱前面的聖經故事〈耶穌和暴風雨〉的英文內容，完成下列的填空遊戲。

1 They pushed the boat from the shore and raised the s_____l.

2 The man at the t_____l tried to steer the boat, but he couldn't.

3 Suddenly a f_____e wind began to below.

4 Jesus heard their cry for help, he saw the lightning f_____h!

5 The boat sailed on the s_____g path that the moon made on the water.

6 "Don't be afraid when the thunder c_____s, I am with you always," says Jesus.

7 Jesus helpers u_____ed the boat.

8 "Lord save us; we p_____h! "they cried.

8 A man sat in the back of the boat to guide it with the s_____g tiller.

8 Jesus stood in a boat-a fishing boat with o_____s and a sail.

Part2

請根據Part1的單字，完成下列的連連看。

B	A	C	K	O	A	R	S	G	X	W	M
O	F	I	E	R	C	E	T	L	C	A	T
O	L	W	I	C	K	L	E	D	H	F	S
T	A	C	S	A	I	L	E	B	W	P	A
H	S	B	R	U	S	I	R	A	V	G	U
Y	H	R	E	A	T	T	I	L	A	B	L
O	P	T	I	N	S	E	N	R	Q	U	P
R	C	E	U	N	I	T	G	R	E	X	E
S	P	A	R	K	L	I	N	G	A	C	R
R	E	U	S	E	O	F	M	A	S	T	I
F	I	L	M	F	L	E	A	B	O	A	S
M	A	R	K	E	T	S	C	R	A	S	H

▍解答見394頁

(The crossword answer grid shown inverted at bottom):

解答

393

Word Search Puzzles

請參閱前面的聖經故事〈耶穌與孩子們〉的英文內容，完成下列的縱橫字謎。

▌解答見393頁

Across （橫）

2 The little girl was so sick they carried her in a h_____k. Jesus said, "Be well, little girl." She sat up and smiled.

4 Moneychangers were c_____g their money, it didn't seem like a Temple at all.

5 There was no sound of singing and praying; instead, there was a r_____y noise.

7 They h_____d the cattle and the sheep out of the Temple.

Down （直）

1 They shouted out loud, "Buy cattle and sheep for your o_____g."

2 A boy with a hurt leg came h_____k, Jesus put His hand on the hurt leg and made it well.

3 The blind man's eyes were t_____t shut, he had never seen anything. Jesus made his eyes see.

4 The boy threw away his c_____g, now he could walk and run!

6 T_____s had brought to the Temple cattle and sheep to sell.

7 Jesus raised His arm and said,"Take These Things h_____e ."

Word Search Puzzles

請參閱前面的聖經故事〈大麥餅與魚〉的英文內容，完成下列的縱橫字謎。

|解答見396頁

Across （橫）

2 Jesus put His hand into the basket and a_____s there were loaves and fishes.

5 Little Lad saw the p_____e look on Jesus' face.

7 When everyone had eaten, Jesus said, "Gather up the l_____r food."

9 Little Lad h_____d home to tell his father and his mother how Jesus had fed a bid crowd of people.

10 He thought, "there is not e_____h lunch for all these people in my little lunch basket."

Down （直）

1 Little Lad c_____d the baskets of leftovers. "1,2,3,4,5,6……12 baskets!"

3 What a s_____e —and all from his little lunch.

4 How many loaves were there in Little Lad's lunch basket?

6 Jesus was asking the b_____g. Little Lad bowed his head.

8 Who brought Little Lad to see Jesus? A_____w

Crossword Puzzles

Part1

請參閱前面的聖經故事〈上帝潔淨大地〉的英文內容，完成下列的填空遊戲。

1. Almost all of the people were w_____ed, many of the animals were fierce.
2. Build the ark of cypress wood, and d_____b it with pitch within and without.
3. They could be g_____r pitch to daub the ark.
4. Then someone on the edge of the crowd p_____ed toward the forest.
5. Noah w_____ed the people about the flood that God was sending to wash away earth's wickedness.
6. The animals m_____ed as in a parade, up the ramp, through the doorway, into the ark.
7. Bullocks d_____ed the logs into the green valley.
8. God told Noah about the f_____d He was sending.

Part2

請根據Part1的單字，完成下列的連連看。

W	O	R	K	W	E	G	J	P	S	U	N
E	L	E	T	R	O	N	I	M	N	R	G
A	F	L	O	O	D	Z	D	A	A	B	W
R	O	O	F	Y	A	X	Z	R	C	Z	Q
E	A	R	T	H	U	W	I	C	K	E	D
D	R	G	U	A	B	N	A	H	A	I	W
G	A	P	W	O	N	D	G	E	R	B	G
R	H	D	R	A	G	G	E	D	Q	C	A
E	N	O	U	E	R	W	H	X	E	N	T
A	H	K	X	G	H	N	X	B	T	Y	H
T	O	P	O	I	N	T	E	D	P	U	E
S	E	A	R	C	H	E	O	D	W	M	R

解答見395頁

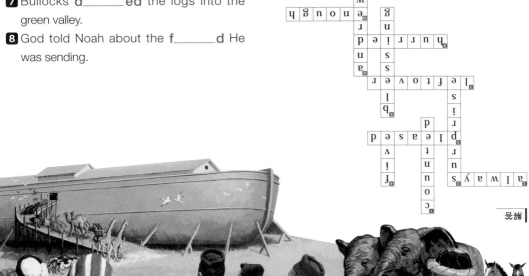

解答

彩圖聖經故事第 / 愛達・戴高凌（Etta B. Degering）
作；Robert Berran 等繪者；蔡依珊譯 -- 初
版 .-- 臺北市：時兆，2015.02
　面；　公分 .--（親子家庭叢書；5）
中英對照
ISBN 978-986-6314-53-7（精裝）
1. 聖經故事　2. 繪本
241　　　　　　　　　103020688

書　名	彩圖聖經故事（My Bible Friends）
作　者	愛達・戴高凌（Etta B. Degering）
繪　者	Robert Berran
	Fred Collins
	Manning de V. Lee
	William Heaslip
	William Dollwick
譯　者	蔡依珊
審 訂 者	李斌祥

董 事 長	李在龍
發 行 人	周英弼
出 版 者	時兆出版社
客服專線	0800-777-798
電　話	886-2-27726420
傳　真	886-2-27401448
地　址	台灣台北市 105 松山區八德路 2 段 410 巷 5 弄 1 號 2 樓
網　址	http://www.stpa.org
電　郵	stpa@ms22.hinet.net

總 經 銷	商業書店　聯合發行股份有限公司　電話：886-2-29178022
	基督教書房　電話：0800-777-798
網路商店	http://store.pchome.com.tw/stpa
電子書城	http://www.pubu.com.tw/store/12072

責任編輯	周麗娟、王姿驊
文字校對	徐雲惠、由鈺涵
封面設計	時兆設計中心　馮聖學
美術編輯	時兆設計中心　馮聖學
法律顧問	洪巧玲律師事務所　電話：886-2-27066556

Ｉ Ｓ Ｂ Ｎ	978-986-6314-53-7
定　價	新台幣 420 元　美金 16 元
出版日期	2015 年 2 月 初版 1 刷

Original English edition copyright ©2008 by Review and Herald® Publishing Association.